LEAD

MW01616173

Discover

THE POWER OF
FORGIVENESS

by
Edith Bajema

FAITH
ALIVE.
Christian Resources

Grand Rapids, Michigan

As far as the east is from the west,
so far has he removed our transgressions from us.

Psalm 103:12

Unless otherwise noted, Scripture quotations in this publication are from
the HOLY BIBLE, NEW INTERNATIONAL VERSION, 1973, 1978, 1984,
© International Bible Society. Used by permission of Zondervan Bible
Publishers.

Cover photo: PhotoDisc

We welcome your comments. Call us at 1-800-333-8300 or e-mail us at
editors@faithaliveresources.org.

ISBN 978-1-59255-212-2

10 9 8 7 6 5 4 3 2

Contents

To the Leader. 4

Introduction. 6

Additional Note to Leaders 7

Glossary of Terms 8

Lesson 1
The Power of God's Forgiveness 10

Lesson 2
The Response of the Forgiven Heart 21

Lesson 3
How Many Times?. 32

Lesson 4
The Hidden Power of Forgiveness. 43

Lesson 5
Stories of Forgiveness 54

Lesson 6
The Good News: Receiving and Giving Forgiveness 65

What Shall I Say?. 77

Evaluation Questionnaire

To the Leader

Prepare the Lesson

This leader guide is meant to assist you as a small group leader, not to substitute for your own personal work. As you prepare to lead each lesson, work first through the questions in the study guide. Then use the leader material to enrich your understanding of the passage.

To avoid giving the impression that you have an answer book or that you know all the answers, we recommend that you not take the leader guide to the Bible study session. After all, the answers are in the Bible, and you are a guide to help your group find the answers in God's Word.

Prepare thoroughly before each group session so that you can lead without frequent references to notes. This approach will free you to concentrate on leadership responsibilities, keep eye contact with group members, and listen carefully.

Get Ready to Lead

Learn to think in terms of questions. As you prepare to lead a lesson, ask yourself questions and try to discover the answers yourself. This will prepare you to anticipate group members' questions and thus help others discover truths from God's Word.

Lead with Questions

Use questions to direct the group discussion. Draw out positive contributions by asking questions. Break down difficult or unclear questions with smaller, concise ones. Also use questions to respond to wrong or problematic answers. If you learn to lead others to truth by questions, you will be a good Bible discovery leader. The questions in this study are designed to be used with the New International Version of the Bible, but other translations can also be used.

Help to Apply

Gently help group members discover the meaning of God's message for their own lives. Be careful not to be judgmental of persons who may not yet seem to be applying the truths you encounter together. It's the Spirit's work to apply God's Word to people's hearts. Tactfully let the group know how the Spirit is applying the Word in your own heart and life. Pray faithfully for the Spirit's work in others.

While giving people the time and space to apply biblical truths as the Spirit leads them, simply try to help group members see that there is a relationship between the Bible and life. Questions for reflection at the end of each session invite everyone to take some time for personal reflection and optional sharing. Try to offer at least a few minutes for reflection time toward the end of each lesson, and encourage group members to do follow-up reflection at home.

Leadership Training

If more than one group in your setting is using this Bible study, we strongly encourage leaders to meet regularly for discussion of the lessons, for prayer, and for mutual support.

If this study is being used in a Coffee Break Small Groups program, each leader should have a copy of the *Coffee Break Evangelism Manual with Director's Handbook*. This book is a basic "how-to" guide for establishing and leading a Bible discovery group. Reread the book or portions of it periodically and review it at the beginning of each season.

Leaders will also find it helpful to attend one or more of the many leadership training workshops offered each year in connection with small group ministry.

For more information,

- call toll-free 1-888-644-0814, e-mail smallgroups@crcna.org, or visit www.smallgroupministries.org

- call toll-free 1-800-333-8300 or visit www.FaithAliveResources.org (to order materials)

Introduction

Someone has done you wrong. Maybe you have been hurt more than you care to admit. The memory of the hurt feels like a wound in your spirit, a deep cut that remains tender and bleeding, though perhaps weeks, months, or even years have passed.

You try not to think about it too much because it makes you feel sad or angry. You may forget about it for days or weeks on end—until you're reminded of that person again. Suddenly all the hurt and anger come to the surface, and the memory of your hurt is as fresh as on the day it happened.

Against that person your heart remains angry, bitter, and confused. How could your friend or coworker or family member or neighbor have wronged you that way? What can you do to show that person how his or her actions made you feel? How can you teach that person a lesson in return?

If you have thoughts like these, a root of bitterness is growing and thriving in your heart. Sometimes a root of bitterness, an unforgiving spirit, will grow until it kills a relationship that once flourished. Sometimes it grows large enough to kill the spirit of the person who harbors it. It becomes a prison, and those caught in it are unable to free themselves.

There is a key that will open the prison and free your spirit. It's the key of forgiveness. It will bring you into the light, into the open spaces of God's love. You will find healing and discover that others are unexpectedly blessed by the change in your heart.

Come and sit by God's side during this study and look into the deep places of the Lord's forgiving heart. Listen to Jesus talk to his friends about forgiveness. See how members of the early Christian church were taught to get along with each other in spite of their differences. Then open your heart to discover the healing power of forgiveness in your own life.

Recommended Resource

It will be clear by the end of this study, if not already, that a six-lesson study on forgiveness can only begin to answer some of the tough questions on forgiveness. One excellent resource is Lewis Smedes's *The Art of Forgiving* (New York: Ballantine, 1997). You may find it helpful to read Smedes's book side by side with this study, as it expands on many questions that group members may ask.

Additional Note to Leaders

Be prepared if any group members indicate that they want to forgive someone but aren't sure how to go about it. Because every situation is different, this study can't begin to give a full description of what the situation might look like, but it's important that you suggest a next step. Here are some ideas of how you might do that:

1. Don't press for specifics, but do ask questions to determine the level of injury sustained: Was this more than a one-time occurrence? Was pain inflicted intentionally and within a close relationship? Is there a refusal to reconcile or even an outright denial that it happened? Is the person who inflicted the injury no longer living or unable to participate in the process? Is the level of injury severe? Was a crime committed?
2. If the answer to any of these questions is yes, then suggest that the person seek help from a pastor, a Christian counselor, a legal counselor or attorney, or a professional mediator. Give specific information about whom to contact and how to contact such an advisor. If at all possible, let your group member make the contact. Offer your ongoing support as the person starts the process. Pray with this person.
3. If the injury caused is not at a high level and if the person who caused the injury is open to meeting with your group member, suggest that they meet together. You'll want to recommend that this meeting take place with the help of a mediator or support person. The goals of the meeting would include
   - communicating the offense and the impact it has had on both parties and on their relationship.
   - opportunity for a response and explanation by the person who caused the offense.
   - an expression of regret and apology for the wrong behavior.
   - a sincere request for and extension of forgiveness.
   - a commitment to doing what still needs to be done to restore the relationship.
   - prayer seeking God's help and guidance in continuing toward reconciliation.
4. If the level of hurt is only one of annoyance, suggest that your group member confront the person responsible either in person or by letter, state the grievance clearly, and ask for an apology. If an apology is received, then the group member can simply say, "I forgive you from the heart." Both parties can then express their joy in reconciling and look for ways to be sure the offense won't happen again.

Glossary of Terms

denarii—A denarius was a Roman coin worth about a day's wages for a laborer in New Testament times (see NIV footnote on Luke 7:41). A hundred denarii would be worth a few dollars in our society today (see NIV footnote on Matt. 18:28).

grace—undeserved favor, kindness, and love. We are saved by God's gift of grace alone through faith in Jesus as Savior (Eph. 2:8).

holy—pure, set apart in a special way to bring glory to God.

hyssop—a Middle Eastern plant that has a long stem and small, white flowers. The Israelites used hyssop to sprinkle blood or water during times of spiritual purification and cleansing (see Ex. 12:22; Lev. 14; Num. 19; Ps. 51:7).

iniquity—sin; refers to one's life being out of balance because God's law has been broken.

kingdom of heaven—God's active rule over the creation that becomes visible wherever places, people, and relationships are devoted to obeying the Lord Jesus Christ. Can refer both to the angels and spirits in heaven and to people on earth who seek to live the way God intended.

mercy—compassion, kindness that is not deserved; often used in reference to forgiving a debt.

Pharisee—a member of the Jewish religious sect that emphasized the importance of religious laws and rituals. Some Pharisees were known for their legalism and hypocrisy.

prophet—one who speaks for God or comes with a message from God.

righteous—free from guilt or sin. God considers people who are joined to him by faith as righteous through Christ.

sin—disobedience to God; conveys the image of a broken relationship with God.

talent—a measure of gold or silver in New Testament times. A talent would be worth more than a thousand dollars in our society today (see NIV footnote on Matt. 25:15), so the ten thousand talents in Jesus' parable of the unmerciful servant would be worth more than ten million dollars today (see NIV footnote on Matt. 18:24).

tax collector—a local citizen who served the Roman government by collecting taxes from fellow citizens. Tax collectors were despised as traitors and often grew rich by paying themselves generously from the money they collected.

transgression—sin; refers to crossing over a line or boundary set by God for obedience.

uncircumcision—the state of not being circumcised. Circumcision was the physical sign of belonging to God's covenant people and symbolized cutting away sin from one's life.

Lesson 1

Psalm 103:1-12; Proverbs 20:9; 1 John 1:9;
Psalm 130:3-4; Colossians 2:13-14

The Power of God's Forgiveness

Introductory Notes

Your preparation to lead this lesson should begin well before the first
week of the study. As soon as you make the decision to lead this Bible study,
you should begin to pray about it.

Why? You will be dealing with things in this study that go deep into the
human spirit—issues of hurt, grief, bitterness, loss. Your group members
may be struggling with trying to understand why they are called to forgive
people who have hurt or betrayed them. They may also be struggling to
understand and accept God's forgiveness of them.

So begin by praying for your group members (even the ones you don't
know) before you meet face to face for this study. Pray that God may be
softening their hearts even now, plowing up any hard ground of
resentment, tossing out stones of bitterness, watering them with showers of
the Spirit's presence and life. If you do this, you will find that seeds you
plant together in your discussions—seeds of forgiveness, healing, and
freedom—will take root more quickly than if you didn't. The Lord wants to
work through your prayers to do powerful things in each person's spirit.

Pray also that you may grow through this study. It's a rare Christian—
even among mature believers—who does not harbor a hidden resentment.
And many of us do not think daily with gratitude about the amazing,
forgiving love God pours on us. Even if you have years of experience as a
group leader, the Spirit can make a tremendous difference in your walk as a
Christian through this study.

While leading this first lesson, do not be afraid to share whatever
struggles you may have with forgiveness. This will open the door for group
members to talk freely about their own questions and hurts.

So begin on a personal note. Talk about your feelings in leading a study
of this kind, and about your anticipation of the Spirit's work in your own
life as you look at the Scriptures together. Acknowledge that you are dealing
with a difficult topic, one that's intertwined with emotion and memory, one
that will touch each person on a personal level. But also emphasize that the
Bible passages you are studying contain truths that form a solid
foundation—truths that bring freedom and healing if they are embraced.

Also become familiar with the good news material at the end of lesson 6
in this guide. Through this study, some group members may be seeing the

God of forgiveness for the first time, and they may become ready to make a commitment to Jesus Christ even before they get to lesson 6. If so, your preparation ahead of time will help you better be able to lead them to faith in Christ.

Optional Share Question

Note: The optional share question in each lesson may serve well at the beginning of your session, or it may fit better at some other time during your discussion. Use or adapt each share question in a way that works best for your group.

What person do you trust most in your life? What makes a person easy to trust?

1. **Psalm 103:1-5**

   a. *What is the psalm writer encouraging himself to do?*

   The psalm writer—in this case, David, who was king of Israel about a thousand years before Christ—opens with three of the most familiar words in all the psalms: "Praise the Lord."

   - **What is included in praise?**

   Talk about the elements of thanksgiving, of telling good things about God, of speaking to God in a spirit of worship and adoration.

   - **What part of himself does David address?**

   Look at the terms David uses: "soul," "all my inmost being." David is speaking of the deepest part of himself. He wants to be stirred in the very heart of his being with praise to God.

   - **What's the difference between praising someone with your mouth and praising someone from the deepest part of your being?**

   - **What difference do you think that makes to God?**

   - **What does the writer challenge himself to remember?**

   God has done some wonderful things for David, and David is concerned that he not forget them.

- Why is it easy to take for granted what someone else has done for us?

- What does this say about us?

If you have a group of seasoned believers, you may want to discuss briefly how easy it can be to take for granted the many blessings and provisions God brings our way. *How many days go past, for example, in which we neglect to thank God specifically for the great gift of salvation?*

Encourage the group's discussion of these verses of Psalm 103 to set the tone for the rest of the lesson by focusing on God's love, compassion, forgiveness, and healing power.

b.   What benefits has the psalmist received from God?

With your group make a list of the benefits David has received from God.

- What has happened to David's sin? To all his diseases?

- What did God do for him when his life was "in the pits"?

Look at the word *redeem* in verse 4 and talk about what that means. To redeem something is to pay a price for it and buy it back, to save something from destruction.

- What does this imply about God's desire to restore and care for a broken life?

- What is David being crowned with?

- What does this tell us about God?

Discuss how wonderful it is that God offers us love and compassion even though we are sinners in need of forgiveness.

Look also at verse 5 and talk about how God has fulfilled the writer's desires.

- What did God give—even when the psalmist may have desired the wrong things?

- What was a result of the good things God gave?

2. Psalm 103:6-10

a. How does God show compassion?

This psalm makes clear that God cares for people.

- **What is God's response when people are oppressed?**

You may want to share with group members who may not be familiar with the Bible that the Old Testament contains God's commands and guidelines for the people of Israel and that many of these commands deal with issues of justice and taking care of people who are weak, unprotected, and helpless.

Much of the Old Testament also tells of the relationship between God and the people of Israel, whom God chose as his own. Encourage group members to read more of the Old Testament, starting with Genesis 11:10, if they are unfamiliar with the history of the Israelites and how God made promises to bless them and care for them so that all nations could be blessed through them (Gen. 12:2-3).

Verses 8-10 are a beautiful description of God's nature. Look at the positive qualities in these verses: *compassionate, gracious, slow to anger, abounding in love.*

- **Does the description of God in verse 8 match your ideas of who God is? How is it the same or different?**

Take note that some of your group members may not have this concept of God.

b. How does God respond to people when they sin?

Though we are sinners who deserve God's judgment, we learn from this passage that God is "abounding in love" and compassion, willing to forgive. While it's true that God does get angry with us and may even deliver much-deserved punishment at times, God is overwhelmingly gracious and long-suffering. If God treated us "as our sins deserve" (Ps. 103:10), we'd have been destroyed long ago, with no hope of salvation (see Gen. 2:15-3:15).

- **Do you think God has the right to accuse and repay? Why or why not?**

- **Why might God choose not to repay, according to this passage?**

13

As you lead, be aware of the Holy Spirit's presence, and rely on the Spirit to reveal to group members the unexplainable and life-giving love that God bears for all of us.

3. Psalm 103:11-12

   a. How great is God's love toward those who fear God?

These are two of the most reassuring and awe-inspiring verses in the Scriptures. They speak of infinite distances, lengths that cannot be measured—all in reference to God's love and forgiveness toward us.

Ask group members to imagine they are standing outside at midnight, looking up at a clear sky full of stars.

- **How high do the heavens actually extend? Is this distance measurable?**

Even today with the help of high-powered telescopes, scientists are unsure how far the universe extends.

- **What does this tell us about God's feelings for all who are in a close relationship with God?**

You may want to read from Ephesians 3:17-19, which puts the same idea into different words:

I pray that you, being rooted and established in love, may have power, together with all the saints, to grasp how wide and long and high and deep is the love of Christ, and to know this love that surpasses knowledge. . . .

As your group is talking about the extent of God's love for them, silently pray this prayer from Ephesians for them. Ask the Holy Spirit to fill their hearts and awaken their desires to taste and see God's love for them.

Take some time to explore the meaning of the phrase "those who fear him" (Ps. 103:11). Talk about the kind of God being described here.

- **Is it likely that *fear* means being afraid of God in the sense of living in terror of God's anger? Explain.**

Note with your group that when the Bible speaks of fearing God, it refers more to respecting and revering God than being afraid. We must have a healthy respect and reverence for God, obeying and serving God with all our heart. As we recognize God's holiness and almighty power and recognize that God holds back from destroying us for our sins, we can see how our relationship with God involves a measure of respectful fear—but God does not hold us in terror. As 1 John 4:16 puts it, "We know and rely on the love God has for us. God is love."

- **What does this suggest about the kind of relationship God wants to have with us?**

b. *What happens to the transgressions of those who have this kind of relationship with God?*

Not only is God's love immeasurable to those who fear the Lord, but so is the extent of God's forgiveness.

Before talking about this marvelous forgiveness, you may want to look briefly at what the phrase "our transgressions" implies about God's people.

- **Do even those who fear God with all their heart break God's laws? Explain.**

It may be comforting for some people in your group to hear again that believers who have a living relationship with God are still as much in need of forgiveness as everyone else. The phrase "our transgressions," implying that we all sin, can in a small way be a comfort for someone who wonders if he or she could ever be "good enough" to have a relationship with God.

- **Is it possible to say how far the east is from the west? Explain.**

If any of your group members have traveled around the world, they've experienced how big our planet is and how vast it can seem to us tiny human beings. But can the distance from east to west ever be measured? Help everyone see that the psalm writer is talking about an infinite distance here.

- **Have you ever felt that a wrong thing you have done has come back to haunt you again and again, hanging over your head or weighing on your conscience?**

- **What does this verse say about that burden? About the extent of God's forgiveness?**

Some group members may have had the experience of being reminded of past wrongs by people who haven't forgiven them—or perhaps by people who never seem to tire of picking at others and accusing them of doing wrong. Though it can be difficult for people to forgive and forget the sins of others—as well as their own sins—we can trust that the Lord completely removes the sins of all who repent and believe in God's power to save. God has "removed our transgressions from us" (Ps. 103:12) through Jesus Christ, who died "once for all" as the sacrifice for sins (Heb. 10:10).

4. *Proverbs 20:9*

    a. What does this question imply about all people?

    b. Do you believe there is anyone who can truthfully say this? Why or why not?

This little saying in Proverbs 20:9 highlights one of the Bible's major themes. Another way to put it is found in Romans 3:23: "All have sinned and fall short of the glory of God."

This verse from Proverbs may start some lively discussion in your group, particularly if you have a number of newcomers or spiritual seekers. It's embedded in our (sinful) human nature to believe that if we try hard enough, we can be good enough for God.

But avoid getting drawn into a useless argument over people's often misguided ideas about sin. Simply state what Scripture says: all people have at one time or another broken God's commands for daily living.

Since this verse in Proverbs asks a rhetorical question, you may wish to ask group members if they know what a rhetorical question is. If anyone is unsure, explain that a rhetorical question is asked in such a way that the answer is clear to everyone.

- **What's the obvious answer to the question in this verse?**

Note also that there may be people who don't see this as a rhetorical question, people who might even say, "Yes, that's me! I am clean and without sin!"

- **What kind of person might say this?**

Many of the Pharisees in Jesus' day thought they could keep God's law perfectly and earn the right to say that they were sinless before God (see Luke 18:11-12). But Jesus easily pointed out their hypocrisy and poor leadership in which they often misled people into thinking they could keep the law perfectly (Matt. 23).

- **Why is this a particular temptation for people who see Christianity mainly as a set of rules?**

Help your group see that if we look at the Christian faith as a set of rules for sin management rather than as a relationship of trust with God, we soon become either self-righteous do-gooders or people who despair of ever being good enough to win God's love and approval.

The only person who ever was and is without sin is Jesus, who kept God's law perfectly. And he gave his life to pay for our sin so that we could be forgiven and considered righteous in God's sight (Rom. 8:1-4; 2 Cor. 5:17-21; Heb. 4:14-16).

5. *1 John 1:9*

   a. *How does this verse echo Proverbs 20:9?*

In this statement the apostle John acknowledges the truth of the human condition—that we are all sinful. (Also see 1 John 1:8.)

- **What does this say about the person who says, "I have kept my heart pure; I am clean and without sin"?**

   b. *What comfort is there in this verse?*

The comfort John emphasizes here, as we will repeat often throughout this study, is that *God forgives.* God waits to forgive; God's heart is ready to forgive; God forgives our many sins and removes them infinitely far from us.

- **What words describe God in this verse?**

Look at the word *faithful.*

- **What does faithfulness mean in the context of our discussion on forgiveness?**

Help group members see that God's promises always hold true; if God has promised forgiveness when we confess our sins, then God will forgive. We can depend on God's forgiveness 100 percent of the time for 100 percent of our sins.

Look also at the word *just.*

- **How does being just describe God in this context?**

- **Do you think God forgives only his favorite people and not others?**

You might point out that God is so just that he could not forgive sins without someone having taken the punishment for sin. So Jesus, the Son of God, took our punishment upon himself.

When we realize that we are not able to keep our hearts pure and we admit this to ourselves and to God, something more happens.

- **What else does God do besides forgiving us?**

Look together at the promise to "purify us from all unrighteousness."

- **What's the difference between someone who says, "I have kept my heart pure," and one who says, "God has purified my heart"?**

6. **Psalm 130:3-4**
   a. *What does verse 3 imply about all people? About God?*

Again, note that the question in verse 3 is rhetorical. Because all of us are sinners, none of us could stand blameless before God.

- **What does the word "if" in this verse tell us about God?**

God not only removes our sins infinitely far from us, as we've learned from Psalm 103:12, but God also keeps no record of our sins. Take a moment to explore this wonderful truth with your group.

- **How does it feel to live with or work for a person who keeps a record of every wrong thing you do?**

- **What kind of attitude does that suggest?**

Talk about the discomfort of being in relationship with such a person.
If you have time, compare this to a statement about Christian love in 1 Corinthians 13:5. Note the parallels to what we've been learning about God's love: "not easily angered," "keeps no record of wrongs."

   b. *What quality of God allows people to have a relationship with God?*

Look again at Psalm 103:8-12 to reemphasize that God wants to have a relationship of love with us. God's forgiving nature allows this relationship to begin and grow.
Note also the word "feared" in Psalm 130:4. This verse makes a connection between fearing the Lord and being forgiven. (See also Ps. 103:11.)

7. **Colossians 2:13-14**
   a. *How does verse 13 describe the condition of people before they were forgiven by God?*

The picture here is one of being dead in sin.

- **What can a dead being do for itself?**

- **How does this describe the hopeless fight of all humans against sin in their lives?**

When it comes to freeing our human natures of sin, we are helpless. We cannot truthfully say, "I have kept my heart pure." That's an impossible task.

You may note—especially for newcomers—that circumcision was a procedure done to all Jewish males in the Old Testament as a sign that they belonged to God. Non-Jewish men who wished to become part of God's people also had to be circumcised.

- **If circumcision was a sign of relationship with God, how does the word *uncircumcision* describe people who were trapped in their sinful nature?**

Such people could not say, "I belong to God"; their sins stood in the way of their having a relationship with the holy and just God.

b. What did God do for them? How?

In Colossians the apostle Paul is writing to people who have recognized their sinful condition and have trusted God to forgive them through faith in Christ. They are no longer dead; they are alive! Though their physical appearance remains unchanged, there's a complete renewal of their spiritual condition and their relationship with God (see 2 Cor. 5:17).

- **What has happened to their sins?**

They are forgiven!

- **How has God accomplished all this?**

- **What happened to the code?**

- **Who took it away?**

- **What did that cost?**

Prior to Jesus' death on the cross for our sake, the old "written code"— that is, the law God had given the people of Israel in the Old Testament— had demanded punishment for sins. The people could bring an animal to be killed as a form of payment for their sins (Lev. 16), but as Hebrews 10:4 explains, "it is impossible for the blood of [animals] to take away sins." But when Jesus, the sinless Son of God, came and offered up his own life, accepting the punishment for human sin, the demands of the written code were satisfied once and for all. God "canceled the written code" on our behalf by accepting Jesus' sacrifice as full payment for our sins.

- **What does this tell us about God's love and care for us?**

Help group members see that not only does God have a heart that's ready to forgive, but God also provided the way to make forgiveness possible. Use this discussion to present the good news of Jesus' gift of life for us through his death on the cross—especially if any group members may not have heard it before.

Questions for Reflection

   a. *What do these passages tell us about the human condition? About God?*

   b. *What is the key to a restored relationship with God?*

These questions should help summarize the basic truths of this first lesson: God's loving and forgiving nature allows us to have a relationship with God. This concept is the foundation for understanding how we, in turn, are called to forgive others. So be sure that your group has had ample time to explore these passages and questions.

Invite group members to participate in the closing prayer by offering brief sentence prayers of thanksgiving to God, if you think they'd be comfortable doing so. If your group includes a number of newcomers, simply offer a brief prayer of thanks for the Scriptures you've studied together during this lesson—passages that offer us great promise and hope as they reveal God's love and forgiveness.

Perhaps your discussion today has alerted you to the needs of group members who may be struggling with forgiveness, or guilt, or the notion of a judgmental God who delights in punishing people for sin, or perhaps another related issue. If so, pray especially for them during the coming week, asking that God may use the Scriptures of this lesson and the power of the Holy Spirit to reveal God's loving heart and desire to forgive and save us.

Lesson 2
Luke 7:36-50; Psalm 32:1-7

The Response of the Forgiven Heart

Introductory Notes

One of the most important things to learn about forgiveness is that our ability to forgive others hinges on our own response to God's forgiveness. The secret to the Christian's ability to forgive is expressed in the words of a simple praise song: "Freely, freely you have received; freely, freely give."

To put it another way, if we take God's forgiveness out of the picture, the command to forgive others doesn't make much sense. Sure, we could probably make a case for the benefits of letting go of resentful feelings, and we could probably identify the negative effects—both physical and emotional—of harboring anger in one's heart. But we'd still be bewildered about why forgiving others is a good and just thing to do.

That's because our ability to forgive others flows from a forgiven relationship with God. God paid a terrible price for our sin—even before any of us turned to God and repented. Because of Jesus' self-sacrifice, God offers forgiveness to the entire world. It's available to anyone who believes in the power of Jesus' death to take away our sins. If we know this God, if we ourselves have found relief in God's forgiving love, if we grow to love this God more and more every day, then forgiveness begins to make sense. We can forgive because God forgives us (Col. 3:13). "We love because he first loved us" (1 John 4:19).

How do we respond to God's forgiveness? Do we take it for granted and perhaps think about it only occasionally? Or does it awaken in us an overwhelming joy and a great longing to know God better, joined with a humility that remembers how much we owe to God's great love and sacrifice?

Today's lesson talks about people who came into contact with God's forgiving love in the person of Jesus. As you lead your group in today's lesson, focus on how these people responded. Do not force a response from group members, but allow the Scriptures to speak to people's hearts, challenging them to walk with deeper joy and gratitude in a forgiven relationship with the God who forgives.

Optional Share Question

What qualities do you appreciate in a friend? What makes for a good friendship?

1. *Luke 7:36-39*

    a. *Who invites Jesus to dinner?*

As you begin reading this passage, take a moment to explain the role of the Pharisees in Jewish society. Though often looked down upon today for being legalists and hypocrites, they were actually pillars of Jewish society and were highly respected in their day as teachers and as moral examples. In some ways we might compare them to churchgoing people today who try to live as good a life as they can, serving as examples of decent, moral behavior.

- **What's often a spiritual weakness in such a person, one who seems to "have it all together" spiritually?**

- **How might such a person be tempted to say, "I have kept my heart pure"?**

- **What may be the Pharisee's motive in asking Jesus to dinner?**

- **What may be his feelings toward this man who seems to be turning the whole religious establishment on its head with his teachings?**

Note with your group that the Pharisees as a whole were not friendly to Jesus. They resented his popularity as a teacher and were skeptical of his miracles.

    b. *Who enters as an uninvited guest? What does she do?*

Though there are many people at the dinner, this story focuses mainly on three. Look for a moment at the woman.

- **What makes the woman stand out from everyone else in the room? How is she described?**

- **What do you think "sinful life" means?**

You might note that in Jewish society, saying a woman had lived a "sinful life" was another way of saying she had loose sexual morals. This woman could well have been a prostitute.

- **How does that set her apart from the other guests in the room?**

Note that it's likely that most or all of the others in the room are men.

- **What risks might this woman be taking as she enters the Pharisee's house?**

- **What does this tell us about the strength of her motivation and desire?**

- **What is it about Jesus that draws her into that house? Causes her to weep?**

This is a key question; take a few minutes to explore it with your group. It's apparent that the woman has had some contact with Jesus before. Perhaps she heard him speak to a crowd. Perhaps he has even talked with her before. Your group should see that at least one thing that draws this woman is Jesus' loving acceptance and forgiving spirit. Though Jesus clearly taught against sin, he was a favorite at dinner parties with "sinners" and religious outcasts of Jewish society (Luke 15:1-2).

- **Why did such people flock to Jesus, when he taught and upheld the same law the Pharisees did?**

Look for a moment at the fact that the woman is crying.

- **What is it about Jesus that may have caused this emotion?**

- **What does the woman bring with her?**

Apparently she does not come to the Pharisee's house on a whim; she has taken the time to purchase a jar of perfume at great expense.

- **What does she do to Jesus' feet?**

- **What do you think this means to her? To Jesus?**

Note that it was a custom in Jesus' day to offer a guest water for foot-washing; the roads were often dry and dusty, and everyone's sandaled or bare feet were often dirty. Explain too that it was a servant's role to wash the feet of guests. Jesus himself would later wash the feet of his own disciples, teaching them to be servants to each other (John 13:1-17). So what this woman is doing is an act of humility and reverence.

c. *What is the Pharisee's response? What does this suggest about him?*

The Pharisee's thought, "If this man were a prophet . . ." indicates skepticism and a touch of enmity toward Jesus. Many Pharisees felt the same as Simon did; Jesus freely criticized them in public, and they longed to discredit him and destroy his popularity.

- **What hint does this give about the reason for inviting Jesus to dinner?**

The Pharisee has likely invited Jesus in order to test him, to try to catch him in a mistake or a false move. (See Matt. 19:3; 22:15-46; Luke 10:25.)

- **Why might Simon feel that this scene gives him a chance to prove Jesus wrong?**

- **What do we learn about Simon's attitude toward the woman?**

Note Simon's judgmentalism and lack of love. He sees this woman in only one light: as a lawbreaker and "sinner" who is not to be associated with.

- **In contrast, what does Simon seem to feel about his own moral status?**

2. *Luke 7:40-43*
   a. *What story does Jesus tell?*

This is one of Jesus' shortest parables. Yet there is much we can draw from it by relating it to the scene that has just taken place in Simon's dining room.

- **How do the two debtors in Jesus' story differ from each other?**

- **How are they alike?**

There's a great difference between the amounts owed to the moneylender. One person owes about two months' wages, and the other owes ten times that amount.

- **If Jesus is talking here about Simon and the woman, whom do you think is represented by the person who owed only fifty denarii?**

- **Which person in Jesus' parable might have thought he might still be able to pay off the debt on his own?**

- **What does this tell us about Simon and his debt of sin before God? The woman and her debt?**

A key point in this parable, regardless of the amounts owed, is that the two debtors are in the same boat. They are dead broke. Neither one has any hope of repaying the moneylender.

- **What does this tell us about Simon, as well as about the woman?**

- **Are Simon's efforts to keep the law able to keep him free from guilt before God?**

- **What question does Jesus ask of Simon as he closes the story?**

The question Jesus asks introduces an unusual twist. One might expect him to ask, "Which of the two will feel more grateful . . . or relieved . . . or indebted?" But instead Jesus asks which one will *love* the moneylender more.

- **Why might someone who views a relationship with God as a set of rules find this question irrelevant?**

b. What does the story tell us about forgiveness?

If group members dig deep, they will discover some insights into what God's forgiveness is like. Consider using the following questions to help:

- **In what ways are there differences in what we "owe" God?**

- **In what ways are we all alike?**

- **What is God's view of our debt once God says, "I forgive"?**

- **What does Jesus suggest about God's motive in forgiving us?**

- **What kind of relationship does God want with us?**

3. *Luke 7:44-50*
   a. How does Jesus apply the story to Simon? To the woman?

As you discuss these verses, make a list together of the ways Jesus contrasts Simon's behavior with that of the woman.

- **What does Simon's behavior reveal about his heart?**

- **What does the woman's behavior reveal about her heart?**

- **How does this relate to the story that Jesus has told about the two debtors?**

Help group members see that Jesus is linking forgiveness with a response of heartfelt love.

- **How is it that Jesus can say to the woman, "Your sins are forgiven"?**

Make sure newcomers in your group know that Jesus, as the Son of God, is speaking for the Father when he tells the woman that all her sins have been forgiven. As true God, Jesus has the right to do this. The religious leaders at Simon's dinner party recognize right away that Jesus is doing something that only God can do (Luke 7:49).

- **What does their response suggest about their view of Jesus?**

b.   What does this story tell us about the response of the forgiven heart?

This story has a happy ending: the woman goes away fully forgiven.

- **But what about Simon and others like him?**

Look with your group at Jesus' words in Luke 7:47: "He who has been forgiven little loves little."

- **What does Jesus mean by this?**

- **What danger does Simon face when it comes to God's forgiveness?**

Help your group see that the person who feels he or she has little to be forgiven (like the one who says, "I have kept my heart pure") does not much value the gift of God's forgiveness. Such people do not understand the perilous situation they are in. They do not see that theirs too is a debt that cannot be repaid, no matter how much they try to follow rules and legalities. They are in danger of missing God's forgiveness altogether—and of missing the greatest love relationship humans can know.

4.   Psalm 32:1-2

a.   What kind of person is blessed, according to these verses?

This psalm gives a personal testimony of one who has received God's forgiveness.

- How do you think the psalm writer is feeling as he writes?

- What is the tone of these verses?

The writer sounds confident, glad, almost jubilant. He's been forgiven, and he wants to share this good news with everyone.
Look with your group at the word *blessed*.

- What does it mean to be blessed?

This concept is often unexpressed today—especially in much of the public media—so take some time to explore its meaning. To be blessed means to be given a gift, to be shown favor. Another translation of the Hebrew word for "blessed" is "happy." Some of our dictionaries describe blessedness as being blissful, joyful; enjoying spiritual happiness.

- Why might this be a good description of a person who is forgiven by God?

b. *How does the writer describe the meaning of forgiveness?*

Look at the three word pictures the writer uses to describe forgiveness: *transgressions forgiven, sins covered, sins that are not counted.* How do these pictures help us understand what it means when God says, "I forgive you"?
Note that the writer does not say, "Blessed is the person who never transgresses, who has never sinned."

- What is assumed here about the human condition?

c. *Why do you think the writer mentions deceit here?*

The writer's mention of deceit raises some interesting questions. At first we might think this statement doesn't follow logically from the one preceding it. But look at it closely together and reflect on why the psalmist might mention it.

- What is often the first instinct of a child who has disobeyed a parent?

- What do people try to do when they have done something wrong?

"I didn't do it!" is often the child's protest to try to avoid punishment for doing something wrong. Even as adults, we try to cover up our wrongdoing and hope no one finds out. But deep down we know that if we've done wrong, we really can't hide our guilt.

- **How does this situation change after confession and forgiveness?**

Help your group see that the writer is speaking of the blissful, joyful condition of someone who no longer has something to hide, someone whose conscience is free and clear.

5. *Psalm 32:3-5*

Some group members may find it difficult to relate to the powerful emotions in these verses. But these are the words of someone who has done something that he knows is wrong in the eyes of both God and other people.

Discuss what kind of sin might make a person feel that way—an extramarital affair, a type of addiction, a dishonest business decision, physical or sexual abuse of another, a death or injury caused by drunk driving, or even intentional murder. It appears to be a shameful act, something that one would never want another person to know about. Talk about the feelings of remorse that could accompany such an act and the desperate desire to cover it up so that others wouldn't find out.

a.   What had the writer kept silent about?

Note with your group that the writer of this psalm, King David, had a close walk with God and a deep respect for God's law. Yet more than once in his life David gave in to sinfulness and acted shamefully (see, for example, 2 Sam. 11:1-12:25; 24:1-25). Whatever David is writing about in this psalm, no one besides he and God knew the whole story of his sin. Eventually God convicted David of the guilt of his sin, and he was brought to confession and forgiveness. But the period of silence and unrepentance must have been excruciating.

b.   How does the writer describe his condition during this time?

Look closely at a few of the phrases in this passage.

- **What happened to David physically because of his emotional and spiritual state?**

- **How does a guilty conscience affect the health of one's mind and body?**

Some people in your group may recall times when they have been troubled by a guilty conscience. Feel free to talk about your own experiences here as well. Your group members may not feel comfortable enough with each other at this point to talk about such personal issues, but your doing so can encourage them to follow your example as the study progresses.

- **Whose hand was on David? How did it feel to him?**

- **What do you think this means?**

David's conscience tormented him—and he realized that it was God's hand at work in him.

- **What does this tell us about the role of the conscience?**

Romans 2:15 points out that even people who do not have a relationship with God are aware of God's laws: "They show that the requirements of the law are written on their hearts, their consciences also bearing witness, and their thoughts now accusing . . . them." Again you might share an example from your own life in which God used your conscience to convict you that you had done wrong.

c.   *What changed this situation?*

Something drastically changed this painful situation for David.

- **What was the catalyst?**

- **What did David have to do?**

- **What does this say about the healing power of truth?**

It wasn't until David was able to leave behind his pride—his defensiveness, his excuses, and his desire to cover things up—that he was freed from his torment. When he could bring himself to say honestly, "I did wrong; I should not have done that, and I'm sorry," he found relief and forgiveness. He had walked from darkness into light.

Take a moment to discuss how important it is to "come into the light" spiritually. Jesus, speaking to Nicodemus in John 3:19-21, gives us a profound revelation of the human spirit:

> "This is the verdict: Light has come into the world, but men loved darkness instead of light because their deeds were evil. Everyone who does evil hates the light, and will not come into the light for fear that his deeds will be exposed. But whoever lives by the truth comes into the light."

- **How does this relate to David's struggle? To our own?**

Acknowledge that it is very hard to bring to light something we're ashamed of having done. But, as David points out, this is the only way to healing.

- **What are the alternatives?**

Talk about some consequences of refusing to confess wrongdoing: one could live with the agony of a guilty conscience or perhaps kill the conscience's voice and lose regard for right and wrong. Recognize here that some group members may be struggling with a sin that they have not confessed to God. This may be a crucial point of decision in their relationship with God—or perhaps a block to their ability to forgive others. Be sensitive to the Spirit's work in their lives and pray for the wisdom to ask the right questions and to know how to encourage strugglers in their spiritual growth.

Psalm 32 itself is very encouraging.

- **What was God's response to David's confession?**

- **How quickly did David receive forgiveness?**

The forgiveness is instantaneous. Note that it seems as though God was waiting all along for David's confession, ready to forgive.

- **What does this tell us about God?**

- **How might it encourage people to confess wrongdoings more readily?**

6. *Psalm 32:6-7*
   a. *What changes in one's relationship to God when a person confesses wrongdoing? Why do you think this happens?*

David encourages the godly person (one who has come into the light and found forgiveness) to pray to God.

- **What is prayer?**

Some group members may think of prayer only as asking God for things we want. Explain that prayer is intimate conversation with God in which believers tell God their deepest desires and needs, speak to God of their love and their trust in God's greatness and power, bring the needs of others to God, and listen for God's direction—through the conviction of the Spirit and through Scripture.

- **Why is this kind of conversation with God impossible when there are unconfessed sins?**

b. What does God become for such people?

People who are trying to hide their wrongdoing might not think of God as a safe place, as a refuge. A guilty conscience can make people think of God as an angry judge, someone they should hide from (as Adam and Eve did after they sinned—Gen. 3:8-10).

- **How does that change once confession and forgiveness have taken place?**

- **How does the psalm writer describe God in these verses?**

Once the guilt is cleansed and the relationship of love is restored, God is the safest refuge anywhere—a hiding place in times of trouble.

- **What attitudes toward God are expressed in these verses?**

Talk about the trust, love, and confidence in God that permeate verses 6-7.

- **How does forgiveness make all of this possible?**

Questions for Reflection

a. What do these passages teach about God?

b. What do they reveal about those who have received God's forgiveness?

Use these questions to review the passages you've discussed and to invite group members to share insights they've discovered. Hopefully your group will focus on the forgiving nature of God and the love and trust that grow in the heart of the one who is forgiven. Be alert for signs that a group member may be struggling to accept God's forgiveness personally, and invite any who may have further questions to stay and talk, if they wish.

Above all, pray—not only for persons who may think their sins are too big for God to forgive, but also for those who, like Simon, may feel they do not need to be forgiven much. Ask God to rekindle awe, deeply felt gratitude, and love for the forgiveness of a debt we cannot repay.

Lesson 3
Matthew 18:21-35; Ephesians 4:32;
1 Corinthians 13:4-7

How Many Times?

Introductory Notes

In the previous two lessons we have focused on God's forgiving nature in order to lay a foundation for forgiving others, such as our neighbor, spouse, coworker, friend, family member—anyone who has hurt us. Jesus makes a direct correlation between receiving God's forgiveness and offering forgiveness to others. His insightful parable in Matthew 18 teaches about the insignificance of others' debts to us compared with our debt to God. If God does not withhold forgiveness from us, how can we withhold it from others?

Optional Share Question

What does it mean to "go the extra mile" for another person? Under what circumstances would you consider doing that for someone?

1. *Matthew 18:21-22*

   a. *What question does Peter ask Jesus?*

Peter seems to be asking Jesus a reasonable question here. Most of us have had someone in our lives who has been a repeat offender, who has crossed the line many times and hurt us again and again. And we may wonder, *How many times should we keep forgiving?* Is there a limit, a time when we say, "Enough! You have crossed the line too many times, and I can no longer forgive you"?

The religious teachers in Peter's day did declare a limit, stating that forgiving a person three times was all that the law required.

   b. *What appears to be Peter's attitude toward forgiveness?*

   • **How does Peter's offer go beyond the law?**

   • **How might he feel about that?**

Help people see that Peter may think he is being rather gracious here. Perhaps he is even looking for an approving comment from Jesus, such as "Wow, Peter—would you really forgive your brother that often?"

But let's look more closely at Peter's attitude toward forgiveness.

- **What would happen after his limit had been reached?**

- **What kind of relationship might Peter have with someone after the eighth offense?**

- **How does Peter's attitude mirror our own limits?**

- **If we set limits, what are we afraid of?**

Talk about the fear of being taken advantage of, the fear of somehow encouraging others to keep offending because they know we will always forgive.

- **What other reasons may we have for putting limits on our forgiveness, even when the offender is sorry?**

- **Have we ever said (or thought), "You don't deserve it!"?**

c. *What is Jesus' answer?*

Jesus' answer must have taken Peter by surprise.

- **What number does Jesus suggest?**

Note with your group that Jesus' answer can also be interpreted as "seventy times seven." Explain that in Jewish thinking the number seven signified completeness; it was often associated with God, with perfection. That may be why Peter chooses the number seven as his limit.

d. *What do you think this means?*

- **What would Peter and other Jewish listeners understand from Jesus' answer?**

Jesus is saying, "Forgive to infinity."

- **What does it say about the true nature of forgiveness?**

- **What does God consider the limits of forgiveness?**

Look again at Psalm 103:12, discussed in lesson 1. If you have time, briefly explore with your group this peculiar perspective God has on forgiveness.

If we understand Jesus rightly, it appears that God will keep forgiving the person who sins, whenever forgiveness is sought—to infinity!

- **What does this tell us about God's heart?**

- **What comfort does this offer us?**

You may wish to look again at Psalm 32:6-7, which we discussed in lesson 2 in connection with prayer, confession, and finding refuge in God.

2. *Matthew 18:23-27*

a. Why might Jesus feel a story is needed here?

In response to Peter's question, Jesus had just made a rather startling statement about the limits of forgiveness—a statement that challenged even the religious law. Peter's face may well have registered some surprise, even disbelief. No doubt others who were listening would be surprised as well. Jesus, the greatest of teachers, knows that they find his words hard to understand. He also knows the power of a story to illustrate the truth.

b. To what does he compare the kingdom of heaven?

Jesus makes a curious statement as he begins his story: "The kingdom of heaven is like . . ."

- **What is the kingdom of heaven?**

Talk with your group about this phrase to make sure they understand it. Point them to the glossary definition in the study guide. Help your group to see that Jesus is referring to God's active rule over creation in a way that becomes visible when people are devoted to obeying God as the ultimate authority and seek to live life the way God intends. Such people try to see life from God's perspective rather than from a merely human view.

- **What point of view will this story reveal?**

Again reinforce that the Bible is profoundly valuable because it reveals the way God thinks about things. Encourage group members to be open-minded to this perspective as you discuss Jesus' story together.

- **Whom might the king in this story represent? The servant?**

Your group should pick up on the fact that Jesus is comparing the king to God and the servant to those who are in God's service.

   c.   *How much does the servant owe the master? What could happen to the servant?*

The servant owes the king an amazing amount of money.

- **How much would such an amount be worth today?**

A sum of ten thousand talents would equal more than ten million dollars in our society today. Not only would it be impossible for a servant in those days to pay back such an amount, but we might also wonder how a servant could ever come to owe such a sum.

After a number of years, the king decides it's time to settle up, and the servant is called in to give account.

- **Why must the servant's plea seem absurd to the king and all those who are present?**

- **What do his words tell us about his unrealistic expectations of his own abilities?**

Stop at this point and reflect on the meaning behind these events.

- **What kind of debt would people today owe to God?**

- **What is Jesus saying about the size of the debt?**

Our debt before God is beyond comprehending. Saying that we can somehow make things right with God on our own efforts is as absurd as the servant's claim that he can repay a debt of millions of dollars on his own meager salary. It cannot be done. Yet our human perspective is often very different from God's. There are still many people today who might say to God, "I can make it right with you by my own efforts."

- **What is the king's response?**

- **What does the phrase "took pity" imply about the servant's condition? About the king's heart?**

The king sees the full extent of the servant's plight, even though the servant may not. The king's heart appears to be tender, especially for a ruler in that culture and regarding a debt so large. Kings in that day were normally merciless and greedy, angry when their loans could not be repaid, and vindictive to people who couldn't pay.

- **What would surprise Jesus' listeners about this king?**

- **What does this tell us about God?**

- **What does this tell us about life in the kingdom of God?**

d.   What happens to this debt? Why?

The debt is completely canceled. In other words, the king takes the loss. The servant no longer has any obligation to repay the debt. To help everyone see the parallel here with the kingdom of God, ask,

- **What did God do to the debt that human sin had built up?**

- **What is the penalty for this debt?**

Explain that ever since the beginning it was clear that the penalty for sin is death (Gen. 2:16-17). As the apostle Paul put it in Romans 6:23, "The wages of sin is death."

- **How did God take that penalty on himself?**

Again you could refer to Paul's words: "God demonstrates his own love for us in this: While we were still sinners, Christ died for us" (Rom. 5:8).

3.   *Matthew 18:28-31*
     a.   What is the servant's first action after his debt has been forgiven?

When the servant leaves the king's presence, he appears to be on a mission. Jesus implies that this man goes looking for a fellow servant who owes him a small debt that's equal to a few dollars in our society today.

- **What might we expect the man to say to his fellow servant—especially after his audience with the king?**

Most of us would expect the man to tell his fellow servant that his debt is forgiven.

- **What happens instead?**

Not only does the man demand his money back, but he also grabs his fellow servant and begins to choke him, and then has him thrown in prison!

b. *What does this tell us about him?*

- **How does his treatment of his fellow servant compare with the king's treatment of him?**

- **What impression does the king's pardon seem to have made on the servant?**

- **How does his fellow servant's debt compare to the amount he had owed the king?**

The huge difference between the king's behavior and that of his servant is striking, especially considering the huge difference in the debts owed. While a hundred denarii would be equivalent to a few dollars in our society today, remember that ten thousand talents would be equivalent to more than ten million dollars.

c. *How do his actions make others feel? How would you have felt?*

Encourage group members to imagine they were part of the king's court and had seen this servant beg for mercy and receive pardon. How would they feel when they later saw him choke his fellow servant and throw him in prison? Anger, outrage, disbelief—all these would be natural reactions to such behavior.

Also look briefly beyond the story to Jesus' meaning here.

- **What does this scene suggest about the kingdom of heaven?**

- **How does our debt to God compare to others' debts to us?**

Though you'll be discussing this concept again later, invite group members briefly to think about the comparison Jesus is making here. It's central to the point of this parable and to Jesus' teaching on forgiveness.

4. *Matthew 18:32-35*

a. *What does the king do when he hears the news? Why?*

The king is furious and calls the man a wicked servant.

- **How does the servant's behavior fit this description?**

Note that our natural reactions to this man's actions (discussed in the previous section) show that we instinctively sense the evil of this man's behavior.

- **What does the king expect in return for his forgiveness?**

The king's angry question, "Shouldn't you have had mercy on your fellow servant just as I had on you?" tells us that he expects and desires the servant to act more like his master, the king. Not to do so implies an ungrateful spirit, a devaluing of the king's generous sacrifice, and a breach of relationship with the king.

- **What happens to the servant?**

The change in his status is swift and complete. He has not valued the king's sacrificial mercy, so he loses it. The servant receives a worse punishment than he would have received initially, when the king was about to sell him and his family to pay the debt.

- **How is this just?**

Help group members to see that because the servant has rejected mercy, he now receives justice without mercy.
Some people may wonder if God acts in a similar way today.

- **Is our salvation dependent on whether we forgive others?**

Refer to Jesus' teaching in Matthew 6:15, which suggests that we have no reason to expect God's forgiveness if we have an unforgiving spirit. In the final analysis God can even forgive our unforgiving attitude. But God does want us to demonstrate our gratitude for forgiveness by showing mercy and forgiveness toward others.

b. How does Jesus compare this story to the kingdom of heaven?

In Matthew 18:35 Jesus explains the story's deeper meaning in one sentence.

- **What does this story teach us about God? About ourselves? About forgiveness?**

Take time to reflect on Jesus' statement here as a pivotal concept in his teaching on forgiveness. Jesus is explaining that our debt of offense to God far outweighs the debt of anyone's offense to us. We are all in the position of the debt-ridden servant. Even if we had several lifetimes, we could never earn our way to heaven by trying to pay off our debt to God for our sins. Jesus says, in essence, "If you receive this forgiveness from God, how can you hold a grudge in your heart against someone who owes you far less?"

- **What warning does Jesus give?**

Jesus teaches that if someone does not value God's amazing forgiveness, they have opted instead for justice without mercy.

- **What does the phrase "from your heart" suggest?**

- **What does this say about how God forgives?**

5. *Ephesians 4:32*
   a. *What is to be the attitude of Christians toward each other?*

Follow up your discussion of forgiving "from your heart" (Matt. 18:35) by talking about the words in Ephesians 4:32 that describe the believer's attitude toward others: "Be kind and compassionate to one another, forgiving each other."

- **What does it mean to be kind?**

- **Whom do you know that you would describe as kind? Why?**

- **What does kindness have to do with forgiveness?**

Talk about the quality of compassion, noting that it means literally "to feel with" someone.

- **Why is important to try to feel what another person might be feeling?**

- **What does it mean to you when people try to put themselves in your shoes?**

- **How does compassion make it easier to forgive someone "from the heart"?**

If you have time, refer back to Jesus' parable of the unforgiving servant. Note together that forgiveness is able to grow and flourish in the environment of a kind and compassionate heart.

b.   What is to be the basis for their forgiveness?

The writer of Ephesians clearly links believers' forgiveness to God's.

- **What example must Christians follow?**

- **Who sets the example?**

God is always there first, taking on the cost of forgiveness personally and offering forgiveness to people who are still God's enemies (see Rom. 5:8). Once believers grasp the truth of what God has done for them, they are moved to do the same.

- **How does this passage parallel the teaching of Jesus' parable in Matthew 18?**

6.   *1 Corinthians 13:4-7*

a.   How do these verses describe God?

Before you begin discussing this question, read from 1 John 4:16 for the group: "God is love. Whoever lives in love lives in God, and God in him." We usually take 1 Corinthians 13, often called the Bible's great "love chapter," to be a description of how we should live—and so it is. But it is also a marvelous description of God's nature and God's behavior toward us. God is love, and God's love is unconditional. Verses 4-7 of 1 Corinthians 13 give us a powerful look into God's heart.

Help group members understand this by asking what they have learned about God in the previous two lessons.

- **What does God's willingness to forgive tell us about God?**

- **What have we learned about God from Jesus' story in Matthew 18?**

- **How do these verses from 1 Corinthians 13 fit with other passages we've studied on God's forgiving nature?**

b.   What does love have to do with forgiveness?

Look at each positive quality of love listed in 1 Corinthians 13:4-7: patient, kind, humble, selfless, even-tempered, glad for the truth, protecting, trusting, hoping, persevering.

- **What do these have to do with forgiveness?**

Next look at negative qualities mentioned: envy, boasting, pride, rudeness, selfishness, anger, keeping a record of wrongs, delighting in evil.

- **How do these prevent forgiveness from taking place?**

Ask group members if they live or work with anyone who appears to keep track of wrongs. Many people often talk of their grievances and grudges, rehashing old hurts and injustices.

- **What does that tell us about their ability to forgive? About their ability to love?**

c. *What do you find challenging about this passage?*

Use this question to help group members express their personal struggles. No one—not even lifelong Christians—can read these verses without being challenged. Some group members may express frustration; others may have questions. Encourage everyone to take their particular challenges to the Lord in prayer, asking for wisdom and guidance and especially God's love in dealing with any areas mentioned here that may present a struggle for them.

Questions for Reflection

a. *What have you learned about forgiveness in this lesson?*

b. *What have you learned about God? About yourself?*

You may want to note that the passages in this lesson deal mainly with a believer's forgiveness of someone who has asked to be forgiven. They encourage forgiveness of an offender who is sorry and who wants to make amends. Lesson 4 deals with the more difficult question of how to treat people who remain enemies by choice, who do not seek forgiveness and reconciliation.

Note too that dealing with someone who repeatedly causes hurt and then repents—only to do the same again and again—does not call for allowing the cycle of hurt and abuse to go on. One obvious example is that of a woman whose husband becomes angry or drunk and abuses her, either verbally or physically. After the anger clears or sobriety returns, he is genuinely sorry and tender and asks forgiveness—but it happens time after time, with no change. Forgiveness does not say, "It's OK to hurt me over and over again anytime you feel like it." You can forgive someone and still take steps to make boundaries or separations that will allow you the respect and safety you need.

41

Use these reflection questions to find out how group members have grown in their understanding of God and of themselves. They may feel secure enough in the group to talk about particular situations in their own lives that need healing and forgiveness. This is where the "salt" of the gospel can really sting, as it touches raw, bleeding places in our lives. This is also where the gospel displays its greatest healing power. So encourage personal sharing, and offer to talk in private with persons who may have questions they may not want to share in a group setting. Pray that the power of the Holy Spirit moves in all members' hearts to bring them closer to the life-changing, forgiving love of God.

Lesson 4

Matthew 18:15-17; 5:43-48; Romans 12:17-21;
Hebrews 12:14-15; 1 Peter 3:8-9

The Hidden Power of Forgiveness

Introductory Notes

What if someone does not ask to be forgiven? What if that person stubbornly remains our enemy? What does God expect us to do?

This lesson deals with broken relationships that may never be repaired. It focuses on people who are difficult to live and work with. This lesson also draws from a wisdom and power that are deeper than our own, calling for trust in the Judge who promises ultimately to set all things right. This lesson can help us see how God's power is unleashed in our lives when we refuse to harbor grudges and instead pray for God's blessings of love, kindness, compassion, and more for people who offend us.

There's a mystery about the power of forgiveness that cannot be explained by logic or reasoning. It can perhaps only be seen as the mighty working of God's Spirit in the human heart—both the forgiver's and the offender's. Some individuals in your group may even be offended by this mystery and resist it, wanting to hear step-by-step logic and a formula that will produce guaranteed results. This is only human.

But, as the apostle Paul reminds us, the message of the cross—a message of forgiving love offered to one's enemies—seems foolish to human ways of thinking: "The message of the cross is foolishness to those who are perishing, but to us who are being saved it is the power of God. . . . For the foolishness of God is wiser than man's wisdom, and the weakness of God is stronger than man's strength" (1 Cor. 1:18, 25).

Paul also knew that without the Spirit's help such a mystery cannot be understood: "The man without the Spirit does not accept the things that come from the Spirit of God, for they are foolishness to him, and he cannot understand them . . ." (1 Cor. 2:14).

So pray for the Spirit's assistance as you lead your group through this lesson. Everyone will need the guiding of the Spirit to see the wisdom of God's way of dealing with enemies. In preparation, also search your own heart to see if there are questions and struggles of your own that you may need to bring to the Lord in prayer.

Optional Share Question

What's the most difficult thing you've ever had to do? What did you learn from that experience?

1. *Matthew 18:15-17*

   a. *What does Jesus tell his followers to do when another believer sins against them?*

   It's important to clarify whom Jesus is speaking about here.

   • **What does the word *brother* tell us about this relationship?**

   If group members are unsure what *brother* means in this passage, explain that Jesus is referring to people who are fellow Christians, siblings in the family of God. If you have group members who live with an abusive spouse, for example, assure them that Jesus is not referring to abusive relationships or relationships with unhealthy power and control issues.
   Jesus suggests a simple procedure for addressing offenses between believers.

   • **What's the first step? Whom does Jesus ask to make the first move?**

   Jesus' expectation is that the wronged person should approach the one who gave offense.

   • **Why can this be difficult to do?**

   Talk about the courage it takes to confront another person and say, "What you did hurt me."

   • **What do we often do instead?**

   Often confrontation takes more courage than we have, and instead we tell a third party how hurt we were, or we remain silent and let resentment build.

   • **But what's the aim of this first step?**

   Note God's emphasis on healed, loving relationships: "You have won your brother over."

b. What happens when the offender does not want to be reconciled?

Jewish law required that disputes in court involve the testimony of at least two witnesses, and Jesus suggests that this is a wise approach. Such an approach also provides a moderator by including someone not directly involved in the dispute who can listen to both sides and try to help each side hear what the other is saying.

- **What happens if this second step is unsuccessful?**

The process Jesus lays out can eventually involve the larger body of believers, who can hear the offense and offer godly counsel toward repentance and forgiveness.

Of course, there's always the possibility that the offending person will harden his or her heart and refuse to acknowledge wrongdoing—even if the church gets involved.

- **What does it mean to treat someone as "a pagan or a tax collector"?**

Jesus' recommendation here is not as harsh as it may seem. Remember, he associated with tax collectors and reached out with compassion to all kinds of outcasts in Jewish society. As this lesson will show, treating someone as an unbeliever does not mean treating that person unkindly or with a desire to get even. It simply becomes a different sort of relationship, more like one that involves dealing with people outside the community of faith. In other words, "if a fellow church member refuses to listen, treat that person as you would an unbeliever."

- **What does this say about the importance of reconciliation and forgiveness among Christians?**

Jesus places high importance on these things. People who refuse are in danger of breaking their fellowship with the family of God. Such persons should not be shunned but should be shown the way of salvation by means of "speaking the truth in love" (Eph. 4:15).

c. Do you think this is a good process? Why or why not?

Listen closely to group members as they evaluate Jesus' teaching here. Ask questions to help people think through the benefits of resolving offenses between believers this way.

- **How does this process protect both sides?**

- **Why might it be important to approach the matter one-on-one initially?**

- **How does this approach show due respect to the offender?**

Talk about the possibility that the one who caused offense may not be aware of having done so. Jesus wisely suggests that you first let the offender know you've been hurt. This process can help to eliminate gossip and resentments that can occur when you talk about people behind their back. This approach also gives the offender a chance to repent in private and, if possible, to prevent the matter becoming public. This courtesy is exemplary in a world in which people rush to file lawsuits on the smallest pretext.

If the offender remains hardened, however, the presence of other witnesses and a moderator can protect the one who has been wronged. This second step also affirms the truth of what the offended person is saying.

Jesus' suggestion of taking the matter to the church also has several benefits, allowing for other perspectives to emerge and thus to provide enhanced spiritual counsel.

- **Why do you think there is no mention of legal courts?**

- **What does this tell us about matters of offense between Christians?**

Note with your group that Jesus implies that these conflicts are essentially spiritual matters.

- **How does this process give opportunity for forgiveness and reconciliation to take place?**

Group members may well have more questions about what Jesus meant when he advised treating an unrepentant offender as "a pagan or a tax collector." In addition to comments already supplied under question 1b above, the next couple of passages from Matthew 5 and Romans 12 in this lesson help in dealing with that subject.

2. *Matthew 5:43-48*

   a. *How do people normally treat their enemies?*

Look at the popular saying quoted by Jesus in verse 43.

- **Do we see evidence of this outside the church? Within the church?**

Even longtime Christians fall prey to this mindset; it seems instinctive to our human nature. Encourage your group to give examples; you may want to bring to your group meeting some headlines from a recent newspaper that describe this very kind of enmity—continuing hatred between opposing groups or individuals.

- **What's the end result of such a perspective?**

Look at nations torn by perpetual war, cities torn by riots and racial tensions, families torn by hatred and divisions. This way of treating one's enemies leads to conflict and to the death of healthy relationships.

b. How does Jesus want his followers to treat their enemies?

Jesus teaches a way that leads to life and peace, saying, "But I tell you: Love your enemies. . . ." Review 1 Corinthians 13:4-7 (from lesson 3), which reminds us of important qualities of God's love: patience, kindness, hope, perseverance, slowness to anger, and refusing to keep a record of wrongs.

- **How might these qualities affect our relationships with enemies?**

Look too at Jesus' command to pray for one's enemies.

- **What can we pray regarding our enemies?**

Encourage group members to offer as many ideas as they can think of. There are many things to pray for, but note that the greatest blessing we can pray for in someone's life is a restored relationship with God. All other blessings flow from that.

c. What reasoning does Jesus give for this treatment?

Jesus gives a compelling reason for treating one's enemies with love rather than hatred—"that you may be sons of your Father in heaven. . . . Be perfect, therefore, as your heavenly Father is perfect" (Matt. 5:45, 48).

- **In what ways do children resemble their parents?**

- **How do you think God wants his children to resemble him?**

Again reinforce what you learned in lessons 1 and 2 of this study: God always takes the first step in reaching out to people and in offering forgiveness.

- **What does God do for people who are unrighteous?**

- **What does this tell us about God's attitude toward them?**

God is extraordinarily patient with and kind to his enemies.

- **In what ways does Jesus want his followers to be different from others in this world?**

Jesus is teaching that God wants us not to be like the world, but to be like God. The more we are able to model God's heart and soul to the world, the more God's healing power will be unleashed in others' lives.

Take a moment to look again at what Jesus said about treating an unrepentant believer like "a pagan or a tax collector" (Matt. 18:17).

- **How does Matthew 5:43-48 shed light on how we are to treat such a person?**

3. *Romans 12:17-21*

   a. How are Christians to respond to people who do evil to them?

The apostle Paul's words are quite strong here: "Do not repay *anyone* evil for evil."

- **What is most difficult about following this advice?**

Our first instinct is to fight back. We want to hit back when we're hit, and we want to smear the name of someone who has wronged us.

Along with telling us what *not* to do, this passage also recommends positive actions.

- **What are some things believers can do to help keep peace?**

As you discuss this question, note the phrases "if it is possible" and "as far as it depends on you." Talk with your group about some situations that might illustrate this. Without going into too much detail, you could add that in some situations the offending party simply makes it impossible for the believer to be an active peacemaker. When that happens, it may be necessary, at least for a time, to withdraw from contact with the other party while continuing to pray for healing and restoration in line with God's will.

We can pray for those who have hurt us, asking that God will make them want to seek the way of forgiveness. Jesus prayed that way even for those who were nailing him to the cross: "Father forgive them, for they do not know what they are doing" (Luke 23:34).

- **What qualities are needed if one is to live at peace with everyone?**

Again it may be helpful to review the qualities listed in 1 Corinthians 13:4-7. As you discuss ways in which Christians can be peacemakers, talk also about the difference between truly loving one's enemy and being a doormat.

- **Which is Paul advocating here?**

b.   *What is God's role, according to these verses?*

Paul continues by saying, "Do not take revenge, my friends, but leave room for God's wrath, for it is written: 'It is mine to avenge . . .' says the Lord" (Rom. 12:19).

- **In what ways does this require a great deal of faith in God?**

Talk about the degree of trust required of the believer.

- **What comfort does this teaching give?**

Look also at the possible reasons that God might ask us to leave matters of revenge and justice up to him.

- **Who is wise? Who is all-powerful?**

Note that when human anger and revenge combine, the revenge is often more severe than the original offense. It's also possible to take offense when none was intended. Human error often results in imperfect justice. God, who knows all things, knows best how to see that justice is done.

The phrase "heap burning coals on his head" may sound like a vengeful act. But commentators suggest that "burning coals" refers to a picture of repentance. In this context it would mean that heaping kindness on an enemy is often a sure way to make that person feel sorry for what he or she has done. The unexpected kindness can lead to a softening of the heart and to a healing of the relationship.

c.   *What is the ultimate outcome?*

In any case, the outcome affects both the offender and the offended. Note that it is easy to be overcome by another person's evil. If someone treats us with cruelty or disrespect or anger, those same qualities can take root in our own hearts and eventually overcome us. Evil is like an infectious disease that spreads from person to person. All of us, even believers who are saved in Jesus' name, have a sinful nature that clings to us.

But believers, who are being remade in the image of Christ, have a choice. They can choose to overcome evil with good rather than allowing themselves to be overcome by evil.

- **What benefit does this choice offer?**

It strengthens the character of Christ growing within them, as they imitate his love for enemies and his trust in God. It protects them from Satan's scheming in their lives, which aims to overcome their spirits with evil.

- **How does the choice to overcome evil with good affect the believer's enemies?**

Ask group members to recall situations in which evil was overcome with good. Only true faith can give us the patience and strength to make such a choice in line with Christ's character. Faith reminds us that we ourselves have been forgiven much. And faith assures us that God will eventually see that justice is done.

4. *Hebrews 12:14-15*

a.   What should others see in the believer's life and behavior?

As you look at verse 14 together, ask,

- **What is holiness?**

If group members are unsure, look together at the definition in the glossary. Holiness has to do with being set apart for a special purpose. It refers to being clean, free of impurity, ready to be used by God for a special task.

- **How does God's forgiveness through Jesus offer Christians holiness?**

The writer of Hebrews links holiness with living in peace with all people.

- **How does this quality show others what God is like?**

Talk about what you have learned about God's forgiving spirit in previous lessons.

- **How can our relationship with God mirror God's peacemaking spirit?**

Look also at the statement "without holiness no one will see the Lord."

- **How does God intend for people to be made holy and to be drawn to God?**

b. *What happens when a Christian misses the grace of God?*

Verse 15 provides a helpful picture to use in examining our relationships with others: a "bitter root grows up to cause trouble and defile many."

- **What can cause a root of bitterness to grow in someone's life?**

- **Can Christians allow such a root to grow in their lives?**

Speak from your own experiences here, and give examples of how one seed of hurt—perhaps someone's critical comment, perhaps an unfair demotion at work or a spouse's unfaithfulness or a friend's betrayal—can take root in anyone's heart. When that offense is remembered day after day, when feelings of hurt and anger are nurtured, when anger builds inside, what happens to the root? It can grow so large that in some cases it will virtually take over a person's heart, such that all the person can think about it is the offense and how bad it hurts.

- **How can such a root harm or defile many people, besides the person in whose heart it grows?**

Most of us know of at least one person who has allowed a bitter root to take over his or her spirit—and how that can affect the person's relationships with others.

- **What characterizes such a person?**

- **What effect does that person have on a home or work environment? A church fellowship?**

Now turn the discussion to focus on what you've been learning about forgiveness in the past few lessons.

- **How does a forgiving spirit prevent a root of bitterness?**

- How would you advise someone who has allowed a bitter root to take hold in his or her life?

5. **1 Peter 3:8-9**

   a. What qualities are to mark Christian relationships?

Take some time to discuss the qualities mentioned in this passage: harmony, sympathy, love, compassion, humility.

- **Why are all of these important?**

- **How is each quality related to a forgiving spirit?**

- **How is forgiveness difficult if any of these is not present?**

If you have time, focus briefly on the word *humble.*

- **Why is humility needed in order to offer forgiveness—especially to someone who does not deserve it?**

- **How does humility lead us somewhere we often don't want to go?**

- **How does pride often block forgiveness?**

Talk about the difficulty of letting go of the desire to prove we are right and the other person is wrong. Also discuss the need to see our own faults, our own failings, and our own massive debt toward God and others—which God has forgiven—before we can let go of pride and forgive someone who has failed and offended us.

Just as Paul reminded us in Romans 12, the apostle Peter urges us not to repay evil with evil, but with blessing (1 Pet. 3:9)—in other words, sympathy, love, compassion, humility (3:8), and more. You may wish to note that this theme occurs many times in the Scriptures, especially in the New Testament.

   b. What is promised?

We are called to repay evil and insults with blessing so that we "may inherit a blessing" (v. 9).

- **What do you think it means to inherit a blessing?**

Group members may have differing ideas on what this means, but it's clear that one blessing to be inherited is the hidden power of forgiveness—

a power from God that frees, heals, cleanses, and brings life to those who offer it as well as to those who receive it.

Questions for Reflection

a. *What things did you learn from these Scripture passages?*

b. *What did you struggle with the most?*

c. *How might these passages apply to people in your life?*

These questions are simple and practical. It's possible that a number of your group members have held grudges or suffered much at the hands of others in their lives. They may find these passages difficult—especially if trying to deal with past hurts mainly on human terms. Be gentle and understanding in your discussion, recognizing that even seasoned Christians need to keep growing in the grace of God and in the grace-full art of offering forgiveness and love to enemies. Sharing about your own struggles in this area may be helpful for others in the group. Remember also that it's the Spirit's responsibility to bring growth to the spirits of others. Share and offer help where you can, without being forceful, and be content that the Spirit will bring about change in people's hearts in God's time and for God's glory.

If you usually close each session with prayer, use your closing time today to pray about issues that group members may have mentioned while discussing various passages. Ask the Holy Spirit to begin removing any roots of bitterness that have taken hold in your hearts, to transform you into the likeness of Jesus, especially in your relationships with enemies, and to unleash the hidden power of forgiveness in everyone's lives, including those of your enemies.

Lesson 5

Genesis 37:2-8, 17b-28; 41:46-49, 53-57; 42:1-7a; 45:1-5; 50:15-20; Luke 23:32-34

Stories of Forgiveness

Introductory Notes

Talking about forgiveness is one thing, but seeing it in action is another. In this lesson we look at two stories—one from the Old Testament, one from the New—that show what it means to have a forgiving spirit.

These are amazing stories in themselves. But hopefully they will also remind group members of one or two personal stories they may have about forgiveness. Encourage people to tell their stories—and tell your own if you have one. Story is often an effective means for revealing the hidden power of forgiveness.

Optional Share Question

Do you remember any stories your parents or grandparents used to tell when you were a child? How have those stories influenced your life?

1. *Genesis 37:2-8*

   a. *What situations have created a bad relationship between Joseph and his brothers?*

   b. *How do these illustrate underlying problems that can destroy relationships?*

   If we look closely at this passage, we discover a number of interesting details about Joseph's family.

   • **What do they do for a living?**

   • **How many wives of Jacob are mentioned here?**

   • **Are Joseph's brothers older or younger than he is?**

   • **Why does their father seem to prefer Joseph over his brothers?**

   As we look at these details, we can gain a sense of what it may have been like to grow up in this family.

- **What words would you use to describe Joseph's family relationships?**

Several things mentioned in this passage work to create friction in Jacob's (Israel's) family. Note the first hint: Joseph's many brothers come from different mothers, and Joseph himself has a different mother than his older brothers do. This passage tells us that Jacob has at least three wives, and you could note that he actually had four (see Gen. 35:23-26). His favorite wife, Rachel, who was Joseph's mother, died while giving birth to Joseph's younger brother, Benjamin (35:16-20).

Also notice Joseph's "bad report" about his brothers. Though the report may have been truthful, Joseph comes across as being rather smug—as we can gather from his report of his dream. And no one likes a tattletale. To his brothers, Joseph probably seems a rather spoiled and coddled younger child. After all, he was clearly the favorite son of their father's favorite wife.

The richly embroidered coat given by Jacob only worsens the situation. It's easy to imagine Joseph wearing it flamboyantly, knowing it signifies his father's favor and sets him apart from his brothers.

- **What do you think Joseph's brothers feel whenever they see him wearing that coat?**

While the coat (and their father's favoritism) roused the brothers' hatred for Joseph (37:4), the dream he tells them about stirs their hatred all the more (37:8).

- **What does Joseph tell about his dream?**

- **How do his brothers interpret it? What is their response to Joseph?**

Note that Joseph may not be as prideful as he may sound in relating this dream; he may simply be surprised and impressed by such an unusual dream and relate it without thinking.

Clearly this passage reveals many underlying issues that could cause strife in any family: favoritism, jealousy, questionable behavior and tattling, offense taken when perhaps none was intended.

- **Have you experienced similar conflicts in your extended families or with acquaintances?**

Don't push group members for answers, but give an opportunity for people to share if they desire.

- **Why are such offenses sometimes the most difficult to forgive?**

55

2. **Genesis 37:17b-28**

   a. *What plan do the brothers make when they see Joseph coming?*

   b. *What does this tell us about their feelings toward Joseph?*

The relationship between Joseph and his older brothers has been deteriorating, but this incident reveals just how bad it has become. They have begun plotting murder.

- **What name do the brothers call Joseph?**

- **What is uppermost in their minds when they see him?**

Joseph's brothers are still angry about Joseph's dream, in which they appeared as servants to their pampered younger brother. Note that they are also able to recognize Joseph while he is a long way off.

- **What is Joseph wearing that enables them to recognize him?**

- **What must the sight of Joseph's robe remind his brothers of?**

If Joseph had dressed in the regular clothes of a shepherd rather than in the rich robe his father had given him, his brothers might not have guessed it was him till he'd traveled much closer. Instead, the sight of him in the distance stirs memories of their hatred of Joseph for who he is, how their father favors him, and how he has treated them. This gives them an opportunity to plot a way to take vengeance on their hated brother.

- **What do you think it would take to make a person truly want to kill a family member?**

   c. *How do their plans change?*

   d. *How would you characterize Joseph's brothers, based on these verses?*

For some of the brothers, their feelings of hatred are tempered by reason.

- **What does Reuben suggest as an alternate plan?**

- **What does Judah suggest?**

- **What are their motives?**

The brothers surely remember Joseph's earlier bad report about them, and they may well anticipate another such report.

Despite the alternate plans that Reuben and Judah come up with, it's clear that all the brothers have decided to get rid of Joseph. Even if they avoid getting his blood on their hands, they are still responsible for mistreating him and placing him in harm's way.

3. *Genesis 41:46-49, 53-57; 42:1-7a*

If group members aren't familiar with the story of Joseph, the following summary explains what happens to him in Egypt before the events recorded in Genesis 41:46-42:7.

After being sold by his brothers to a caravan of Ishmaelites, Joseph is sold again in Egypt to a government official named Potiphar. Potiphar likes Joseph and elevates him to a place of high responsibility—until Potiphar's wife unfairly accuses Joseph of trying to sleep with her. Joseph is then put in prison, where he proves himself trustworthy to the wardens and becomes known for his God-given ability to interpret dreams. The Bible mentions often throughout this ordeal that "the LORD was with Joseph" (see Gen. 39:2, 21, 23).

After several years, God gives Pharaoh, the ruler of Egypt, a dream about seven fat cows and seven lean cows, and Joseph is summoned to interpret its meaning. With God's help, Joseph is able to warn Pharaoh that seven years of severe famine will come after seven years of abundant harvests. Then Joseph suggests a plan to store up crops during the abundant years so that the people will have plenty of food during the lean years. Pharaoh is so impressed with Joseph's interpretation and his plan that he makes Joseph the second-highest official in the land under Pharaoh himself.

   a.   *What crucial role does Joseph play in Egypt's history?*

   b.   *How does Joseph's importance extend beyond Egypt?*

Without the warning about the coming famine, Egypt—like every other country—might have squandered its resources during the good years and not saved enough for the coming lean years. Joseph's interpretation of Pharaoh's dream—with God's help, of course—makes it possible for Egypt to survive as a nation even through the years of famine. Based on historical information about the population of Egypt and surrounding nations at that time, the number of lives saved during this great famine could well have been hundreds of thousands.

   •   **Who else is saved as a result of Joseph's plan?**

Look at how personal the story becomes. Though many miles and years of separation have come between Joseph and his family, he is being used to save his own family members from starvation.

    c. How is Joseph's dream fulfilled?

- **What hint in this passage reveals that Joseph's position in Egypt is no accident?**

- **What do his brothers do when they come into his presence?**

Help your group see that God has been working behind the scenes in this story. Joseph's brothers bow down to him, just as he had foreseen many years earlier in his dream (Gen. 37:6-7). To care for his people and make them a blessing to all nations, just as God had promised many years earlier to Jacob's grandfather, Abraham (Gen. 12:2-3), God is turning events in this family's history from great evil to accomplish even greater good.

4. Genesis 45:1-5

The following summary explains what happens in the story between Genesis 42:7 and 45:1.

Although Joseph recognizes his brothers, they do not recognize him. So Joseph decides to test their hearts before revealing his identity. He designs an elaborate scheme to get them to bring Benjamin, his younger brother, to Egypt. (Benjamin is now his father's favorite in place of Joseph, who is presumed dead.) Then Joseph tests the brothers to see if they will betray and desert Benjamin as they did Joseph years earlier.

Joseph's plan shows that his brothers have changed. Judah even offers to become a slave in Benjamin's place, pleading with the Egyptian ruler to let Benjamin return to his father. Joseph is overcome with emotion and can no longer keep his identity a secret.

    a. What are Joseph's feelings when he finally reveals himself to his brothers?

Joseph's story is certainly moving. It can be difficult to think of all the years of suffering and homesickness Joseph must have gone through before he found himself face to face with the brothers who had sold him into slavery.

But let's not look only at Joseph's emotions at this point. Ask group members to imagine his brothers' feelings as well.

- **What thoughts are racing through their minds?**

- **What might they be afraid of? Why?**

The brothers naturally become terrified as they realize the tables have turned. Their guilt has been exposed, and now it is Joseph who holds power over them—more power than anyone would have imagined. The memory of the terrible things they had done to Joseph and to their father would again be fresh in their minds. *What would Joseph do to them now? Surely he must hate them!*

    b.   *What attitude does Joseph show toward them?*

Joseph responds far differently than this brothers expect.

- **What does he guess about their thoughts?**

- **What does he say to comfort them?**

    c.   *What role has God played in these events, according to Joseph?*

Joseph is looking at things not only from a human point of view. He sees that God has been working faithfully behind the scenes in all of these events.

- **What reason does Joseph see for his having been sold into slavery?**

- **How does Joseph's faith in God affect his treatment of his brothers? His ability to forgive them?**

5. Genesis 50:15-20
    The following summary explains events that have taken place since Joseph reveals his identity in Genesis 45:1-5.

Joseph brings his father, brothers, and all their families to live in Egypt, providing them room to graze their flocks and flourish in the region of Goshen. Jacob lives for seventeen more years in Egypt before he dies.

    a.   *What do Joseph's brothers fear after their father's death?*

Joseph's brothers seem still to be afraid of Joseph's anger. In a way, their thinking makes sense.

- **Why might Joseph be waiting till his father's death to take revenge on his brothers?**

Joseph loves his father deeply and would surely want to spare him any more grief. But those considerations could change after his father's death, and Joseph might see an opportunity for revenge.

- **What hint do we have that even Jacob may have thought Joseph still had ill feelings toward his brothers?**

The brothers send word to Joseph saying that their father left a message for him: "Forgive your brothers the sins and the wrongs they committed in treating you so badly" (Gen. 50:17).

Note also another detail that hints at the brothers' fear:

- **How do the brothers communicate with Joseph?**

- **Why do you think they send a messenger instead of meeting with Joseph themselves?**

  b. *What does Joseph do when he receives their message? How does he answer them?*

As it turns out, the brothers do not know Joseph as well as they should. Note Joseph's emotions as he receives their message.

- **What do you think causes him to weep?**

Help group members to see Joseph's affection for his brothers, his desire for a restored relationship with them, and his lack of bitterness.

- **What do these qualities have to do with forgiveness, in light of the Scripture passages we have studied in previous lessons?**

After preparing the way with their contrite message, the brothers throw themselves at Joseph's feet.

- **What earlier scene does this bring to mind?**

Joseph's dream is being fulfilled yet again as his brothers declare themselves his slaves. Recall with your group the brothers' mocking words in Genesis 37:8: "Do you intend to reign over us? Will you actually rule us?"

- **How have their attitudes toward Joseph changed?**

Joseph's answer is a lesson in grace.

- How does he acknowledge their sin against him?

- How does he make clear that he will not seek revenge?

Joseph speaks plainly about the brothers' evil intentions toward him, but he also states clearly that it is not his place to take revenge, as he asks, "Am I in the place of God?" (Gen. 50:19).

- What other passages does this remind you of?

Recall with your group the Scripture passages you've studied that challenge us not to repay evil with evil but to remember that God says, "It is mine to avenge; I will repay" (Rom. 12:19; see 12:17; 1 Pet. 3:9).

- What does this say about Joseph's relationship with God?

c. *What does he see as God's role in all this?*

d. *What have you learned about Joseph's character in this story?*

Take a few moments to talk about Joseph's faith in God's ultimate plan for good. If there's time, read with your group a few passages that speak of God's commitment to turn evil to good for those who love God (see Rom. 8:28; Heb. 12:7-11; James 1:2-4; 1 Pet. 1:6-7). The Heidelberg Catechism, a statement of faith written by the early Protestant church, puts it in these words: "I trust him so much that I do not doubt he will provide whatever I need for body and soul, and he will turn to my good whatever adversity he sends me in this sad world. He is able to do this because he is almighty God; he desires to do this because he is a faithful Father" (Q&A 26).

Note that this does not mean we will always be protected from the often painful consequences of another's or our own sin or from accidents that happen because we live in a broken world. But there is comfort and grace for all who love God. What Joseph's brothers did was wrong, harmful, and caused great grief and suffering, yet God worked through it to bring about good.

- What hope does this story give us?

6. Luke 23:32-34

If any group members are unfamiliar with the story of Jesus' life and ministry, the following summary provides some major details.

Jesus, the Son of God, became human and was born to an Israelite girl, a virgin named Mary. At age thirty Jesus began his ministry of working miracles and teaching people about the kingdom of God. After three years Jesus was brought to trial by the religious leaders of his own people. He was condemned on false charges and sentenced to death on a cross—a criminal's death. Jesus submitted to all this willingly, knowing that his innocent death would pay the penalty for the sins of all who would believe in him and receive God's forgiveness.

a.   What is happening to Jesus?

For anyone in your group who may not be familiar with Jesus and the story of his life, death, and resurrection, this discussion provides an opportunity to tell that story briefly.

Our focus in these verses is Jesus' response to the people who have just nailed his hands and feet to the cross. Ask group members to imagine the scene for a moment. Jesus has just come from his trial with the Roman governor, where he was severely flogged and publicly ridiculed. He has been made to carry his own cross through the crowded city streets, and we can assume that those who led him were not gentle. The same men who had spit on Jesus, beaten him, mocked him, and pushed him through the streets now stretch out his arms and nail spikes through his hands. They also push on his legs and drive a huge spike through both feet. Then they set up the cross, with Jesus nailed to it, and drop it into its hole in the ground. The physical pain is excruciating.

What follows is a mystery.

b.   What is Jesus' concern for those who are crucifying him?

Jesus' prayer for the people who are crucifying him shows the heart of God in a way that perhaps no other word or action of Jesus does. Help your group to explore this mystery by discussing the following questions:

- **For whom is Jesus praying?**

- **What have they done to him?**

- **What does he ask the Father?**

Talk about this from a human perspective.

- **What might you or I have done in such a situation?**

It's true that Jesus knows his death has a purpose—that it will bring forgiveness, freedom, and healing to people, opening the way for all believers to be saved from sin. But it's difficult to see why he, the perfect Son of God, should put up with the ridicule and pain of crucifixion.

- **Why shouldn't Jesus become angry with those who treat him with cruelty and disrespect?**

- **What power does Jesus hold as the Son of God?**

- **What could he do to the people who mock him, even as he hangs on the cross?**

- **What does he choose to do instead? Why?**

- **What do Jesus' words tell us about his heart and his thoughts at that moment?**

Despite his extreme physical pain, despite the grief he knows is yet ahead of him, despite the injustice of the soldiers' cruelty, Jesus sees through to their hearts. He knows they do not know who he is. He sees their sin, but he also knows that they have no idea they are killing the Son of God. So he has compassion for them. He does not want them to suffer the death they deserve. He knows that his Father has said, "It is mine to avenge; I will repay" (Rom. 12:19). But instead he steps in between his Father and the people who have mistreated him and asks God to forgive them.

c.   What example does Jesus set for his followers?

- **If we were to follow Jesus' example, what would that mean for us?**

- **Are we capable of doing what Jesus did?**

At this point we must be careful not to demand more of ourselves and others than God does. Jesus' forgiveness was immediate and complete. Our forgiveness of an enemy may take a long time—perhaps even years—and it may never reach the fullness of love and compassion that Jesus showed.

Look again together at Luke 23:32-34 and ask what this passage shows us about God's heart.

- **How does Jesus' prayer contradict the picture that some people have of an angry, vengeful God waiting to punish wrongdoers?**

Earlier in his ministry Jesus said to his followers, "Anyone who has seen me has seen the Father" (John 14:9), and, "I and the Father are one" (John 10:30).

- **What does Jesus' prayer on the cross show us about the Father?**

Again, this teaching may be comforting to group members who from childhood may have been fearful of God's anger at their mistakes and sins. If they learn anything from this lesson or this study, may it be that God is loving, compassionate, full of forgiveness and understanding. Only as we experience this love firsthand are we changed enough to be able to offer love, compassion, and forgiveness to others, even to our enemies.

Questions for Reflection

a. *What have you learned about forgiveness from these stories?*

b. *Do you have any stories from your own life or from the life of someone you know that may teach something about forgiveness?*

Use these questions to review important points from the stories you've discussed and to highlight what you've learned about the nature of forgiveness. Be sensitive to those who may respond to these stories with some anger or impatience; they may be struggling deeply with the need to forgive someone in their own lives. As Lewis Smedes says in his book *The Art of Forgiving*, "Forgiving is a journey; the deeper the wound, the longer the journey." Pray that God will use these lessons to bring to light any wounds that need healing and to begin the healing process for Jesus' sake.

Lesson 6

Psalm 51:1-17; Mark 11:25

The Good News: Receiving and Giving Forgiveness

Introductory Notes

Being a Christian is always a matter of new beginnings. Each day there's a need to say, "Please forgive me for this mistake, for this lack of love, for this addiction, for this unkindness. . . ." There's a need for a fresh start, for being made clean, for pruning dead wood and starting new growth, for replacing ache and despair with hope and a glad heart.

Some people in your group may not yet have had their beginning of receiving the gift of faith in God. Others may need again the reminder of God's love and the freshness of being made clean and holy through God's forgiveness. This lesson gives everyone the opportunity to take God at his word. It offers group members the freedom to experience the cleansing, healing, restoring power that comes when we ask to be forgiven. Each person, whether an unbeliever or a seasoned Christian, can echo David's cry for love and compassion (Ps. 51:1) in the face of personal failings and weaknesses.

As believers receive from God, they can also begin to give to others. Slowly, perhaps—but nonetheless with some new growth in place of the old, dead wood in their lives. There may be a hint that the prison bars of a bitter spirit are beginning to weaken and give way. All this is evidence of God's Spirit at work, so again make prayer a large part of your preparation for this lesson. Ask the Spirit to work in your life as well as in the lives of your group members.

Optional Share Question

What role do you think guilt plays in the lives of people today? What do people do to get free of guilt?

1. *Psalm 51:1-2*

   a. *What is the spirit, or feeling, of this passage?*

   Help group members gain a sense of the tone of this psalm.

   • **How is the writer of this psalm feeling?**

- **What is his need?**

- **What emotions are behind this prayer?**

Humility, grief, longing, hope—all these and more describe the condition of a spirit before God in need of forgiveness. As you progress through this lesson, pray that the Holy Spirit will bring each of you to an understanding of the emotions expressed in this prayer and of your own need for forgiveness.

Before going further in your discussion, make sure group members know the meaning of three key words in these opening verses: *transgression, iniquity,* and *sin.* It's important to understand what the psalm writer is confessing and feeling sorry for. *Transgress* has to do with stepping over a line or boundary that God has set for obedience. *Iniquity* comes from an old word that means "uneven" or "unfair" and implies that one's life is out of balance because God's law has been broken. *Sin,* as disobedience to God, conveys the image of a broken relationship with God.

It may be helpful to remind group members that the entire law of God can be summarized in two phrases: *Love God with all your heart and soul and mind* and *love others as you love yourself* (Matt. 22:37-40).

b. What does this prayer ask God to do?

Group members will be able to identify at least four things that are being requested in these verses: *mercy, blotting out, washing,* and *cleansing.* Look briefly at each of these, exploring what they have to do with forgiveness.

- **What does *mercy* mean?**

Look back to the parable of the unforgiving servant (Matt. 18:21-35), discussed in lesson 3.

- **What did it mean for the king to have mercy on the servant?**

- **In what ways would the one who prays the words of Psalm 51 be in the same position as the king's servant?**

Blotting suggests that God has kept a record of the person's transgressions, as in an account book or ledger. This prayer asks God to blot out, or wipe away, all the transgressions that have been recorded.

- **How would this cancel the debt?**

- **Could the record be read by anyone after it was blotted out?**

You might suggest that to blot out a transgression is the same as having a criminal record expunged by our court system today. All documents are destroyed; the evidence no longer exists.

Washing pictures something similar to blotting out.

- **What does washing away imply about iniquity?**

Talk about the "dirty" feeling people can have after doing something that is unfair, unjust, or out of balance with God's teaching. It can feel as though everyone who looks at us can see the thing we did because of the terrible stain on our conscience. We want desperately to be able to wash that dirty feeling away. That's how the psalmist feels here.

Cleanse implies an even deeper process of washing.

- **What does it take to get a stubborn stain out of a piece of clothing?**

Often the clothing must be soaked, bleached, and scrubbed in order to be completely cleansed. *Deep cleaning* may be an accurate term to use here.

- **How might this apply to a person's sin?**

- **What would it take for a person to submit to cleansing from God?**

The thought of surrendering to God in this way may be a bit frightening.

- **What will God do if we confess we've botched things up and we ask God to take control and make things right?**

- **What reassurance can we find in these verses?**

c. *What qualities of God are mentioned in these verses?*

Look at the qualities of *mercy, unfailing love,* and *compassion.*

- **How do these make confession to God safe?**

- **How does confession require a trust in God's compassion and unfailing love?**

If there's time, note that *compassion* means "to feel with" someone.

- How is it possible that God can feel what it means to be human, and empathize with our weaknesses?

Share with your group the assurance of Hebrews 4:15-16:

> We do not have a high priest who is unable to sympathize with our weaknesses, but we have one who has been tempted in every way, just as we are—yet was without sin. Let us then approach the throne of grace with confidence, so that we may receive mercy and find grace to help us in our time of need.

This is one of the reasons why Jesus, the Son of God, became human.

d. What does this prayer tell you about the one who is praying it?

This is the prayer of a person who sees how far he has fallen into sin and who knows that he must confess it and ask God for mercy and forgiveness.

2. Psalm 51:3-6

a. What is troubling the writer of this psalm?

You might want to mention, if group members don't already know this, that the writer of this prayer is King David of Israel, who slept with a neighbor's wife, got her pregnant, and then had her husband killed (see the note at the beginning of Ps. 51 in your Bible; see also 2 Sam. 11-12). Everything was hushed up, of course, and the king hoped that no one would ever know about it. He was king, after all, and in those days most kings acted as if they could do whatever they wanted.

But this is the same King David who wrote Psalm 103, which we looked at in lesson 1. David was a person who was close to God, and God was not going to let this slip by unnoticed. So God sent a messenger to David to point out what a terrible thing he had done. As David listened to the messenger, he realized how far he had strayed from where God wanted him to be as a king and as a follower of God. David had crossed lines that he shouldn't have crossed, and he made excuses for behavior that could not be excused. His prayer of confession—known today as Psalm 51—grew out of this awareness.

Human sin comes in all different sizes and shapes. Our sins may not be the same as David's.

- How is our situation different from that of the writer of this prayer?

- How is it similar?

b. What does he acknowledge about God in these verses? About himself?

Take a moment also to look at the writer's relationship with God.

- **What place does the psalmist give God in his life?**

- **What does he realize about his sin?**

- **Whom has it hurt the most?**

- **Who has every right to judge and condemn him?**

Note with your group that while David is focusing on his sin against God, that doesn't mean he has not sinned against his neighbor, his neighbor's wife, and all the other people he is supposed to serve justly as king. David is pointing out that he has broken God's law, God's guide for living in all our relationships, so God is the first and the main person against whom he has sinned. And because he has broken God's law, the king has broken the whole law, shattering relationships with all others around him.

If necessary, note again the summary of the law from Matthew 22:37-40, which points out that the first and greatest commandment is to love God and that the second is to love our neighbor as ourselves. Jesus points out that the whole law of God hangs "on these two commandments," meaning that if one or the other of these is violated, the whole law is broken (see also James 2:8-11). And if God's law is broken, God is the one who's offended most of all.

In Psalm 51:5 David also acknowledges something that the Bible teaches in many other places: Sin is bound up in our human nature, and we cannot escape it (see Rom. 3:22-23; 5:12; 7:14-25).

- **How old was David when sin had a hold on him?**

Talk about how sin is a part of our very nature; we are sinful from the time we are born.

c. At what level does God want to work in his life?

Look closely at Psalm 51:6.

- **What has David come to realize, after months of trying to cover up his sin?**

- **Who sees into the deepest places of our thoughts and feelings?**

Talk about the level at which God wants to work in a person's life.

- **What qualities does God want to see in the deepest part of the soul?**

- **How might this change a person's life and perspective on sin?**

3. *Psalm 51:7-9*

   a. What changes does the writer of this psalm ask God to make?

   b. What pictures does he use to describe God's forgiveness?

Psalm 51:7 introduces an important point about cleansing.

- **What is the only way a person can feel clean again?**

- **Who has to do the cleansing?**

Notice the confident tone of these verses: if God does the cleansing and washing, "I will be clean."

- **What does that tell us about God's forgiveness?**

The writer asks to have his dirty conscience cleansed and to be able to feel joy and gladness instead of the crushing weight of guilt.

- **Why is God the only One who can make these changes?**

Read together the explanation about hyssop in the glossary. The mention of hyssop in this prayer would have reminded the people about God's forgiveness. When they sinned and needed spiritual cleansing, they brought a bull or other animal to the priest to be sacrificed as atonement for their sin. The priest would dip a branch of hyssop into clean water and into the animal's blood and sprinkle it on the people to show that God accepted the animal's death on their behalf and that they were now cleansed from guilt.

Group members may find the idea of being sprinkled with blood distasteful, but remind them that at the very heart of the Jewish covenant with God was the idea that sin has to be paid for with blood. As Hebrews 9:22 puts it, "The law requires that nearly everything be cleansed with blood, and without the shedding of blood there is no forgiveness."

You may want to share this with your group as a way of explaining why Christ shed his blood for us.

- In what way do people still need to be "cleansed with hyssop"—in other words, sprinkled with the blood of a sacrifice to be made clean?

- What sacrifice made it possible for all people to be made clean and forgiven?

In 1 Peter 2:24 the Bible says, "[Jesus] himself bore our sins in his body on the tree, so that we might die to sins and live for righteousness."

In a spiritual sense, God dips a branch of hyssop in his Son's blood and sprinkles it on all who come for forgiveness. Hebrews 10:22 says, "Let us draw near to God with a sincere heart in full assurance of faith, having our hearts sprinkled to cleanse us from a guilty conscience and having our bodies washed with pure water."

The psalmist also pleads with God, "Hide your face from my sins" (Ps. 51:9).

- What might this statement mean?

Remind your group of Psalm 103:12, which you discussed in lesson 1: "As far as the east is from the west, so far has he removed our transgressions from us." That, along with the picture of blotting out our sins, suggests that no one will have to see or remember those sins anymore once God has forgiven them.

4. *Psalm 51:10-12*

   a. What hope does verse 10 offer?

Verse 10 is beautiful for several reasons. First, it expresses a sinner's deep longing to be free from continuing struggles with sin.

- What kind of a heart does the psalmist ask God to create in him?

- What does this tell us about his ability to change his own heart?

The desire for a pure heart will bring one closer to God. Jesus said, "Blessed are the pure in heart, for they will see God" (Matt. 5:8).

- What does it mean to have a pure heart?

You might mention that *pure* means "not mixed with any other substance." For example, pure gold has no impurities or alloys in it.

Talk about the possibility of a heart that is wholly filled with love for God and the desire to follow God's will.

- How would having a pure heart protect against further sin?

- What kinds of things can get mixed in to make a heart "impure"?

Ask your group how God's ability to create a new heart can bring hope to someone who has been struggling with sin.

- What does it mean to have a steadfast spirit?

Talk about the need to be able to stand firm when temptations try to pull us from following the will of God.

b. What is the writer's concern regarding his relationship with God?

David's concern over his relationship with God illustrates one of the side effects of sin.

- How does sin affect one's relationship to God?

- What could be the end result if sin is not confessed and forgiven?

Romans 1 gives a graphic picture of what happens when people refuse to acknowledge God and God's law, when they "do not think it worthwhile to retain the knowledge of God" (1:28).

- What does a restored relationship with God bring?

First it brings joy, a joy that comes from being free at last from feelings of guilt and shame. It also brings "a willing spirit," a spirit that wills to serve God so that the believer's walk with God can be sustained in God's strength.

5. *Psalm 51:13-17*
a. What happens to someone who has been forgiven by God?

Verses 13-15 describe a person who is exuberant, vibrant, ready to talk about the deliverance and forgiveness God has given.

- What has such a person been delivered from?

- What does that person talk about with others?

- Who hears this good news?

Note also that the psalm writer asks God, "Create in me a pure heart" (v. 10) before being able to teach others about God.

b. *What does God really value?*

Verses 16-17 might have taken some Israelites by surprise. God had given many laws regarding sacrifices to bring as sin offerings, and those sacrifices were required of all God's people.

- **Why would the writer say that God takes no delight or pleasure in such offerings?**

- **What is God really after?**

Look at what God does take pleasure in. Talk about the difference between going through the motions of saying "I'm sorry" and truly being sorry for what you've done wrong.

- **Why would God value the one far more highly than the other?**

Use these questions to reinforce an underlying theme in Scripture: God wants us to know how much he loves us, and God wants us to love him back. Rituals and religious observances aren't the main thing; God wants our hearts.

6. Mark 11:25

a. *What must we be aware of when we pray to our Father, according to Jesus?*

b. *What happens when we offer forgiveness to someone who has offended or hurt us?*

c. *How does this verse relate to Jesus' story of the unforgiving servant?*

This brief verse summarizes much of what we've been discussing in this study. Because God forgives us so freely and lavishly, so eagerly and with such great love, we must offer that same forgiveness to each other. Jesus did not say it would be easy. He simply said we had to do it.

Be sure to relate this verse to Jesus' parable of the unforgiving servant (Matt. 18:21-35) in order to put things in perspective. Recall together your discussion of this parable in lesson 3.

In addition, as we learned from the story about Simon and the prostitute (Luke 7:36-50) in lesson 2, the person who may feel that his or her debt wasn't much for God to forgive is also the least likely to show mercy and forgive others. We need to have a sense of how deeply God has forgiven us; otherwise we become like the unforgiving servant and the judgmental Pharisee.

This is not to say that we always have to think about how wretched and corrupt we are. There is much that is magnificent and beautiful about being human, for we are created in God's image. But it's healthy to have a realistic awareness of our sin. Sin has permeated our human nature, and we daily fall short of loving God with all our heart and treating others with the love we have for ourselves. A terrible consequence of sin is that it hurts God in the deepest way imaginable. We need to know that we are hurting God and others and that we must ask forgiveness. It's the only way to deal with the reality of our sin.

We also need to forgive others. This does not mean that forgiveness of a wrongdoer must be instantly complete. Forgiveness takes time, lots of prayer, and lots of effort, in God's strength. Avoid giving group members the impression that if they aren't able to forgive completely right away, they are in danger of being condemned. Encourage them to talk with others about the things they need to forgive, to pray about those issues, to tell God about their hurt and pain, and to ask God for the wisdom and courage to let go of their bitterness and love their enemies.

Questions for Reflection

a. How is God's forgiveness related to our forgiveness of others?

b. What have you learned about forgiveness that relates to your own life? Are there areas in which you need God's forgiveness? Are there people in your life you would like to be able to forgive?

Use these questions to allow group members to reflect on what they've learned and to share about any struggles they may have with forgiving and being forgiven.

After everyone has had an opportunity to reflect on these questions and to talk about personal issues, suggest that you spend the final part of your time together in prayer. Remind everyone again of the simple gospel message: that Jesus offered himself as a sacrifice to die in our place so that our sins might be forgiven and we might have a healed, restored relationship with God. Encourage those who have not yet asked for that forgiveness to do so during your prayer time, or later with you privately.

Invite group members who already have a firm faith in God to use this prayer time to bring before God any areas of their lives that need God's correction, guidance, and forgiveness. Encourage people to prune away more of the old, dead wood of sin in their lives and, like David, to ask for a pure heart and renewed steadfastness of spirit.

Also invite members to pray aloud or silently for God's help in forgiving people who have hurt them. Pray for the healing of relationships, for the courage to ask forgiveness if that is needed, and for the Spirit's work to change feelings of bitterness and hatred into compassion and love, even for people who have no desire for reconciliation.

End your prayer time with thanks again for the overwhelming love God offers you through the sacrifice of Jesus and for the complete forgiveness he has provided.

After your prayer time has ended, be sure to find a way, either now or through later follow-up, to offer a listening ear and encouragement to anyone who may need to talk or pray with someone about unresolved issues of forgiveness.

Keep praying about the seeds that have been sown during this study, asking that they may be watered by God's Spirit and may grow into life-giving changes that break down the prisons of bitterness and resentment with the forgiving grace of God.

An Invitation

Listen now to what God is saying to you.

You may be aware of things in your life that keep you from coming near to God. You may have thought of God as someone who is unsympathetic, angry, and punishing. You may feel as if you don't know how to pray or how to come near to God.

"But because of his great love for us, God, who is rich in mercy, made us alive with Christ even when we were dead in transgressions—it is by grace you have been saved" (Eph. 2:4-5). Jesus, God's Son, died on the cross to save us from our sins. And "everyone who believes in him receives forgiveness of sins through his name" (Acts 10:43). It doesn't matter where you come from, what you've done in the past, or what your heritage is. God has been watching over you and caring for you, drawing you closer. "You also were included in Christ when you heard the word of truth, the gospel of your salvation" (Eph. 1:13).

Do you want to receive Jesus as your Savior and Lord? It's as simple as A-B-C:

- **A**dmit that you have sinned and that you need God's forgiveness.
- **B**elieve that God loves you and that Jesus has already paid the price for your sins.
- **C**ommit your life to God in prayer, asking God to forgive your sins, nurture you as his child, and fill you with the Holy Spirit.

Prayer of Commitment

Here is a prayer of commitment recognizing Jesus Christ as Savior. If you long to be in a loving relationship with Jesus, pray this prayer. If you have already committed your life to Jesus, use this prayer for renewal and praise.

Dear God, I come to you simply and honestly to confess that I have sinned, that sin is a part of who I am. And yet I know that you listen to sinners who are truthful before you. So I come with empty hands and heart, asking for forgiveness.

I confess that only through faith in Jesus Christ can I come to you. I confess my need for a Savior, and I thank you, Jesus, for dying on the cross to pay the price for my sins. Lord, I ask that you forgive my sins and count me among those who are righteous in your sight. Remove the guilt that accompanies sin and bring me into your presence.

Holy Spirit of God, help me to pray, and teach me to live by your Word. Faithful God, help me to serve you faithfully. Make me more and more like Jesus each day, and help me to share with others the good news of your great salvation. In Jesus' name, Amen.

What Shall I Say?

This study on forgiveness will likely bring many emotions to the surface. You may well have one or more group members who struggle with grief, perhaps from wounds received long ago. More often than not, you won't be able to solve their problems or "make it all better" by any specific words or actions. As noted in the introduction to this study, problem situations and crises are complex. Grief, anger, and sorrow take time to heal; they must be endured before healing can come. Your most important function will be to listen and sympathize.

Those who are overwhelmed with grief may feel they have no one who understands them. They feel as though they are speaking a foreign language in a community where daily life goes on as usual despite their sorrow. Nicholas Wolterstorff wrote of the isolation of grief in his book *Lament for a Son:*

> I walked into a store. The ordinariness of what I saw repelled me: people putting onions into baskets, squeezing melons, hoisting gallons of milk, clerks ringing up sales. "How are you today?" "Have a good day now." How could everybody be going about their ordinary business when these were no longer ordinary times? I tried to jog and could not. It was too life-affirming. I rode along with friends to go swimming and found myself paralyzed. I tried music. But why is this music all so affirmative? Has it always been like that? I have to turn it off. There's too little brokenness in it. Is there no music that speaks of our terrible brokenness?

Sympathy and understanding are very important to a hurting person. Your responses can make your friend feel the warmth and love that you want to communicate. On the other hand, a well-meaning but thoughtless remark can cut the gulf of alienation deeper than it was before.

The following remarks are commonly offered to hurting people in the hope of making them feel better, but such statements can make the hurting person feel even more misunderstood and alienated. Following each of these remarks is a suggested alternative that can help us better communicate our understanding, sympathy, and love.

1. *I know just how you feel.* Even if you have been through a similar experience, you cannot really know how another person feels, since each individual reacts to stressful situations differently. Instead you might say, "I can see that this is a real burden for you."

2. *It is God's will* or *These things happen for a reason.* Like Job, grieving persons do not need our attempts to explain their suffering. Such a

person may well respond, "If it was God's will to do this terrible thing to me, then I want no part of a God who can be so cruel." Grieving people are not able to comprehend the reason for their suffering. All they know is that they are hurting and confused. Instead say something like "It's hard to understand why this had to happen" and try to show God's love and comfort through your own actions of care and kindness.

3. *Don't cry.* A Jewish proverb says, "Tears are to the soul what soap is to the body." Tears need not be embarrassing. They help to cleanse the soul, release the pain, and relax the tension. A good cry may be just what your friend needs. Assure your friend by saying, "Go ahead and cry. Here's a tissue." If you feel comfortable doing so, hug your friend or hold your friend's hand; this can say more than words.

4. *Try to look on the bright side.* A person caught in the struggle of grief or difficulties is unable to be optimistic. Indicate instead your willingness to listen by saying something like "I'm sure things took pretty dark right now."

5. *At least you have . . . (a wonderful spouse, your other children, good health, or whatever); Look at so-and-so; he's worse off than you are; Things could be a lot worse.* All of these statements belittle your friend's pain. When someone is hurting, confused, or angry, that person is not interested in such comparisons. Instead say, "You are going through a really difficult time."

6. *Everything is going to be fine.* No one can predict the outcome of a hurtful situation. Instead you might say, "I'm not sure how this will turn out, but I'll stick with you and be here for you and pray for you."

Don't try to heal your friend's pain, but do offer freely your presence and love. Above all, listen. This is the best way to show sympathy and understanding. Remember, grieving people can't control the way they are feeling. But your love and sympathy can give them the assurance that they have an ally and can perhaps help them make some progress toward healing.

Evaluation Questionnaire

DISCOVER THE POWER OF FORGIVENESS

As you complete this study, please fill out this questionnaire to help us evaluate the effectiveness of our materials. Please be candid. Thank you.

1. Was this a home group ___ or a church-based ___ program? What church?

2. Was the study used for
   ___ a community evangelism group?
   ___ a community faith-nurture group?
   ___ a church Bible study group?

3. How would you rate the materials?

   Study Guide
   ___ excellent ___ very good ___ good ___ fair ___ poor

   Leader Guide
   ___ excellent ___ very good ___ good ___ fair ___ poor

4. What were the strengths?

5. What were the weaknesses?

6. What would you suggest to improve the material?

7. In general, what was the experience of your group?

Your name (optional) _____

Address _____

8.   Other comments:

(Please fold, tape, stamp, and mail. Thank you.)

Faith Alive Christian Resources
1700 28th Street SE
Grand Rapids, MI 49508-1407